This book is dedicated to:

June Wian
Generous Beautiful Gracious
&
Lola Hansen
God's Gift To Those Who Knew Her

…and to the millions of food service personnel across the country …corner hot dog stand to a gourmet's delight… who really do want you to have a *full* *fill*ing experience.

If the Marriott Corporation presence in the early seventies, and the top executives who contributed to Big Boy's success of the sixties, had Bob Wian's marketing skills they would never have taken the Original Double Deck Hamburger out of the tissue wrap and full color illustrated glassine bag and just... put it on a plate.

Would this "bottom line lunacy" take a Grill off the Rolls Royce, the Golden Arches from McDonald's, the Pillsbury-Doughboy off the biscuit mix, and the Prancing Horse from the Ferrari? Possibly... because their decision eighty-sixed the unique, functional, and persuasive Big Boy presentation Bob created. No more showbiz, geewhiz, and advertising moxie.

One more time. They prepared the most exciting hamburger **recipe** of the century and just... put it on a plate? ...and put Bob's Big Boy, as we knew it, **almost** out of business in California. Sad, sad, sad... sad!

I'm surprised they didn't put the Big Boy in a leotard and work out a co-op advertising campaign with Weight Watchers.

There is, however, another Bob... last name Liggett... who just might turn things around. You'll learn more about the other Bob later... in this report.

CONTENTS

This book is to a large extent the history of the famous Bob's Big Boy, the Original Double Deck Hamburger, but it dwells even more on the life of the man who invented it, Robert Charles (Bob) Wian (pronounced "Y-N"), who revolutionized the hamburger sandwich and the restaurant industry.

Robert Charles Wian, in his time the country's most honored restaurateur, didn't go after fame. Fame found him. And he never felt that the praises wealth brought him were undeserved. A big ego? You bet. But he had a truly sincere desire to see his employees prosper, and he saw to it that they did. He was a man who had style and class.

There were days in the 40's, 50's and 60's when more people ate at Bob's Big Boy than saw all the movies in Los Angeles. He was as famous as Shirley Temple, more popular than Elvis, with an office door that was always open to anyone and everyone who had something to say. Bob was a superstar and built what was without question the finest restaurant chain in America. No one could touch him, and certainly in these times of mediocrity, no one has even come close to the standards for quality food, service, and atmosphere that Bob Wian created and maintained for 32 years in the fast food and coffee shop industry.

Bob was successful and famous, but he lived with a constant anxiety that what he had built might be compromised in somebody else's hands. Unfortunately, his concern became a reality. Bob's Big Boy was simply too big to stay small. To protect his trademark Big Boy, he had to expand, directly or through franchising. Things did indeed get out of his control, and the subsequent loss of control meant a deterioration of the excellence he had worked so hard to achieve. The wolves were out there, and they may have destroyed the legacy of Bob Wian's contribution to the food service industry.

A BOOK IS BORN . . . A THIRTY YEAR PREGNANCY

Material for this book was gathered in the 40's, 50's, and 60's and augmented during recorded interviews with Bob Wian and others in the 70's, 80's, 90's and through 2001. In a taped conversation I had with Bob on May 6, 1970, I suggested to him the idea of this book. Here's how that conversation went:

BOB: "A book about Big Boy? You're kidding! It'll never sell."

CHRIS: "I've been around you and the company for a long time; the great years, all the way to Marriott. It's a wonderful story. What do you think?

BOB: "Well, if anyone can tell it, you can, and it should be told, but it had better have some super photos, or it will put them to sleep."

CHRIS: "We'll call it 'The King and I.'"

BOB: "I think that's taken."

CHRIS: "You're not serious?"

BOB: "Lots of pictures. Lots of pictures."

4

FROM THE DISH ROOM TO THE BOARDROOM

I had known Bob personally as one of his employees. My first job at Bob's Big Boy was in 1946 when I was hired by a big, very pleasant man of about fifty. I learned later it was Bob's dad, 'Pappy'. He hired me for eighty-seven cents an hour as a dishwasher at Bob's No2 in Burbank. My co-worker was Rudy Martinez, who later became Traffic Manager at the massive commissary that prepared and shipped the food to the restaurants each morning. Handsome Rudy and his pretty wife, Nettie, were special to Bob for all the right reasons. Rudy retired with $90,000 in pension trust money from Bob's profit sharing program.

My employment with Big Boy was as follows: dishwasher, 1946; drive-in crowd control, gentleman bouncer, 1949-53; Vice President of Marketing and Board Member of Big Boy Franchises, Inc., 1959-68; Advertising Agency, 1968-70; Franchisee, Big Boy Mobile Systems, Inc., 1968-74. Other positions between Big Boy assignments included; two years at Warner Bros Pictures, four years as Advertising and P. R. Director for the Frito Company (Now Frito-Lay) and two years at Hixon and Jorgensen Advertising, a top west coast ad agency.

In my first few months as a dishwasher at Bob's Big Boy in Burbank, I learned what working for a winner was all about. All the people at Bob's were the best they could be at what they were doing. Bob encouraged them and made them feel that they were an important and necessary part of the team. Occasionally, I would lean down to pick up a bus tray of dirty dishes and find myself looking into the face of a friend or neighbor. Embarrassing? No way! Working for the best and always in the best interest of the customer is a pretty good situation, especially when from the top down every position at Bob's carried with it a feeling of self-respect and dignity.

It was during my time as a dishwasher that I learned that the store manager worked the window. That is, when the waitress or carhop brought in the order, the Burbank manager/window man Harry "Bear" Andrews called out the order to the kitchen. Example: "Big Boy, center out, no rel, add tom," in exact language. In my case, a speech block acquired in 1942 thru 45 during a hitch in the U.S. Navy in World War II made it impossible for me to consider advancing into manager status. I then took full advantage of the GI Bill education package and was later able to serve at Bob's in different capacities.

THAT WAS THEN . . . THIS IS NOW

Bob's Big Boy started in a different era, an era with different values. Drug abuse was extremely rare. Foul language was seldom used in the workplace, and never in the company of women. There were love songs, sad songs, funny songs, but never sick songs. Singers could sing, and you could understand the lyrics the first time around. The evil, the violence, and the sickness in the world didn't come charging at you in your living room, in the movies, or at the grocery checkout stand as they do today. The world was not perfect then, of course, but it was a gentler time—a time when human dignity counted for something. While today's popular values are different, some values of yesteryear are still with us if we choose to embrace them. Many held by Bob Wian are still worth embracing..

Play the Nat "King" Cole recording of the song "Unforgettable," and you'll experience the sense of values we had in the past. You can get the same feeling today when you listen to the 90's version of the same song sung by daughter Natalie Cole and her dad as they captivate a public starving for style and class but really aren't sure where to find it. Most don't know what it is. Style and class—Bob Wian had a ton of both..

Glendale News-Press

WHAT ABOUT BOB'S?

Ex-executive wants to make sure people don't forget their burger roots in Glendale

By Jacqueline Fox, *News-Press*

GLENDALE — Chris Hansen's mission in life is making sure the pudgy guy in the red-checkered overalls be given his rightful place alongside such American icons as apple pie and the Ford convertible.

THE HANSEN FILE

◆ **WHO:** Chris Hansen
◆ **AGE:** 73
◆ **WHAT:** Former vice president of marketing for Bob's Big Boy and author of "Eighty-Six: The Story of Bob Wian and the Big Boy"

What's cookin', BIG BOY?

Las Vegan Chris Hansen pens a flavorful history of that yummy American landmark, Bob's Big Boy restaurant

By Bob Shemeligian
LAS VEGAS SUN

In his southwest Las Vegas home, Chris Hansen has written the great American novel — but the narrative is nonfiction.

And it is as much a part of American history as the mass production of the automobile or the development of the motion picture industry.

Hansen, 73, recently compiled a history — which he hopes will interest publishers — of Bob's Big Boy, the restaurant chain that changed the course of culinary history in America.

A generation ago, the colorful statue of the pudgy, black-haired, hamburger-toting lad was a familiar sight in cities from Las Vegas to Boston. The chain was founded in 1936 in the Los Angeles bedroom community of Glendale

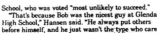
February 1937

School, who was voted "most unlikely to succeed."

"That's because Bob was the nicest guy at Glendale High School," Hansen said. "He always put others before himself, and he just wasn't the type who cared about business or making money."

Wian's classmates were right: The last thing in the world Wian wanted to make was money. What he wanted to make was the perfect hamburger.

Four years after he graduated from high school, Wian sold his old DeSoto for $350, and used the money as a down payment on a 10 stool lunch stand in Glendale. The name of the restaurant: Bob's Pantry.

In Wian's first pamphlet to new employee he spelled out his culinary philosophy: "To serve the best food at reasonable prices and an immaculate restaurant, with courtesy and hospitality."

On most of the East Coast, "Who's Big Boy?"

On all of the West Coast, "Everybody Loves Big Boy?"

LOCAL

Bob's – Where the stars *didn't* come out

Odds and ends from around the Valley:

Had a nice talk recently with former longtime Toluca Lake resident Chris Hansen who had a column I'd written on the glory days of Bob's Big Boy restaurant sent to him by Bob Hope's office.

Hansen, who now lives in Las Vegas, wrote the definitive book on the Valley's most popular drive-in hangout in the '50s and '60s. It was entitled, "Eighty-Six — The Story of Bob Wian and the Big Boy."

Hansen started his career with Bob's in Toluca Lake as a lot man, which is a nice way of saying he was a bouncer. He went on to become vice president of marketing for the popular chain, which grew to 23 restaurants before Wian sold out to the Marriott Corporation in 1963.

Hope — along with movie stars like Mickey Rooney, Debbie Reynolds.

DENNIS McCARTHY

Jonathan Winters, Dana Andrews, Alexis Smith and Craig Stevens — were regulars over at the Toluca Lake and Burbank Bob's drive-ins.

"Bob Hope would use the Burbank drive-in often because it was off the beaten track and afforded him the privacy he desired," Hansen said. "Once in a while, he'd even try out new jokes on me."

Hansen said it was not unusual for carhops at Bob's to work 10 years or more because the tips were good, especially from the movie stars who regularly ate outside in their cars for privacy.

"With seniority you got the best stations," he said. "At Toluca Lake, there were 60 (car) stalls. The station furthest away had six stalls. The closest also had six stalls directly in front of the window or counter from which food was picked up and placed on trays to be taken to the car.

"The No. 1 (in seniority) girl, therefore, walked not more than 20 feet to her customers, while the last girl ran 60 feet to and 60 feet from each car," Hansen said.

"The No. 1 girl at Toluca Lake for many years was Irene Wright, a Joan Crawford look-a-like who didn't know how to frown. She was constantly pursued by the young and not-so-young men about town."

A little-known fact, Hansen says, was that Wian set up a profit-sharing plan for his longtime employees.

"There were veteran carhops who ultimately left the company with benefits exceeding $100,000, some over $300,000," Hansen said. "Looking back on it now, it was a pretty doggone nice life at Bob's."

Yeah, it was.

☐☐☐

If you drove through Chatsworth and parts of Northridge recently, and wondered why there was a red ribbon tied around every fire hydrant, it was to honor the local firefighters of Battalion 15 of the Los Angeles Fire Department.

"It was the community's way of celebrating and honoring them for all the work they do on the job for us out there," said Michelle DeGaetano, who helped organize the event with local neighborhood watch people and Councilman Hal Bernson's office.

"Firefighters don't ask for pats on the back," she said. "This was our way of giving them all one, and letting them know we appreciate them."

Nice touch.

☐☐☐

And finally, for all you parents tired of the politics and backbiting that goes on in too many youth baseball and softball leagues, stop by Hansen Dam Sports Center in Lake View Terrace beginning July 6 for a refresher course on how these youth sports programs are supposed to work.

The coaches instruct, then get out of

the way so the kids can play and have some fun.

The L.A. Kids Sports Academy is sponsored by the city's Recreation and Parks Department with a $234,000 supplemental block grant from HUD. More than 1,000 boys and girls from 98 low-income area rec centers throughout the city are invited to a week of learning and playing baseball and girls' softball.

There will be eight sessions in all, running from Monday through Aug. 27. The program is sponsored by the L.A. Dodgers, the Manny Mota Foundation, Coca-Cola, Panasonic and Aramark.

The kids attending have been chosen by the park directors of their low-income area rec centers. The only criterion was that they had a desire to learn to play baseball and have some fun this summer.

Not a bad criterion for any kid.

Dennis McCarthy's column appears Tuesday, Thursday, Friday and Sunday.

PASADENA STAR-NEWS

Daily News

LAS VEGAS SUN

THE **BIG BOY** STORY

"King of Them All"

artist Roy Grinnell

by Christian Hansen

A 60 Year Association with Bob Wian and the The Big Boy Family

Guy Hansen Family   Lionel Richie   Bonny Abernathy   Billy Graham

John Bacon   Sara Smith   Annette Marroquin   Ronald Reagan

Elizabeth Storm   Bob Hope   Joel Adler   Jack Whalen

Placibo Domingo   Tina Hansen   Jackie Robinson   Ronnie Schell

Leontyne Dean   Barbara Betterman   April Riessen   Tom Gamboa

John Harker   Toto Zara

A good style must have a novelty at the same time concealing its art.
Aristitle; Rhetoric 111.c.322 B.C.

Cathi Bates   John Wooden

Cary Grant   Coiln Powell

Pro West   Bud Rinker   Vern Tyler   Phillys Diller

Bob Jones   Roberta Sutherland   Delce Penfield   Brian Lamb

Lauren Bacall   Dave Hewitt   Cheri Mora   Joe Dimaggio

Dee Baker   Jon Kyle Hansen   Fred Astaire   Michael Caine

Nancy Tooze Hansen   Lisa Foley   Barnaby Conrad   Burt Lancaster

Clark Gable   C. E. Doolin   Walt Disney   John Flynn

William F. Buckley   Miguel Langarcia   Emmy Ewald   Rita Ferri

Kevin Hansen   Ray Walston   Bill Webb   Paul Brinkman

Bob Omens   Dan Bertka   Elanor Thomas   Jill Karniki   Syd Greer

Kevin Bratton   Brooke Phillips   Mike Herbert

Estelle Moreland   Sue Boething   Meryl Streep   Bill and Annie Robinson

Brett Hansen   Jessica Lange   Julie Andrews   Orsen Wells

Jerry Dunphy   Bruce Johnson   Dennis Vetter   Mary Free

Mark Stouffer   Rosemary Neel   Rudy Giuliani   Glenn Mathews

Willie Shoemaker   Wayne Gretsky   Gary Salstrom   John Powls

Dusty Sutton   Carl Gibson   Richarn Scrima   Bob Westberg

Ben Eelle   Don Fagan   Shing Hayashi   Sid Johnston

George Martinez   Lynn Schneider   Roy Andolfo   Bill Milligan

Ron Belden   Merle Van Scyoc   Dick Norris   Jack Catlin

Racheal Clark   Kent Phelps   Lou Fierro   Doug Warren

Jim Koren   Gordon "Pat" Gibbons   John Cummins

Gary Williams   Tom Hill   Rudy Martinez   Joan Woods

Dan Eldredge   Elaine Toledo   Wayne Harville

Carl E. Thornton

Ann Thompson   Marlin Smythe

Roger Poulin

"No money can ever buy class.
You got it or you ain't got it.
Louis Armstrong

Ed Schenkel

Mike Clark   Bill Simone   Tim Roof

Sally Hammons   Dale Dungan

Dick Manley   Ron Chrostowski   Dick Ingham   Reynel Martinez

John Mc Cubbins   Bill Asbury Jr.   Barry Pellssier   Scott Gordon

Don Safian   H. A. Martin   Roger Osgood   Gary Bogstad   Gil Le Fransois

Mike Rigg   Roberta Sutherland   Shirley Mewharter   Ron Novodoczky

Ray Koerntgen   Ron Borden   Dave Lind   Bill Smilor   Betty Fagan

John Heater   Jim Stratemeyer   John Barringer   Roger Mundwiler

Ray Johnston   Donna Odgen   Ed Gokey   Al Robbins   Stan goodman

Dick Mueller   Joel Booras   Louis Walter   Bob Skillsky

Dick Wilks   Ed Wood   Cathy Smith   Bob Roose   Alex Haddad

Bee Gaines   Bill Bellamy   Paul Suminski   John McCaffery

Aurelio Alcala   Ron Milch   Viva Mollenkoph   Don Harris   Robert Eakin

Norm Dyche   Jan Clark

John Van Deventer   Tim Larin

A mans style is as much a part of his face, his figure, or the rhythm of
his pulse. Francois Fenelon: Dialogues des morts. 1712

Bill Botke   Lynne Scinta

Jim Long   Don Deering   Leonard Franklin   Bruce Di Cristina

Nap Alinsod   Mark Mccabe   Don Schumacher   Bob Ingham

Wilbert Hoffman   Wm. Pike   Bob Logan   Bill Rothwell

Fred Stein   Forest Smith   Mike Gillespie   Ruth Dorman

Donald Jordan

9

HOME OF THE BIG BOY HAMBURGERS

Bob's

Famous for
Hamburgers - Chili - Steaks
Thick Malts and Thin Pancakes

Two Locations in
San Fernando Valley

900 East Colo. Blvd. · Glendale
and
624 E. San Fernando Rd. · Burbank

IN THE BEGINNING

Bob Wian was self-annointed to be "the most unlikely to succeed" in his graduating class of 1933 at Glendale High School in California.

[Bob] "I was making nineteen dollars a week with a baby on the way. I'll never forget it. I was washing my roadster in a garage and a sign painter who worked out of the same place said he had just painted a For Sale sign for the little ice-cream parlor down the street. I didn't let my car dry . . . drove it wet down there to look at the place. I bought it. Everybody said, "you're nuts . . . leaving a good job to open a greasy spoon."

In 1936, Bob Wian sold his pride and joy, a 1932 DeSoto, for $300 and bought a ten-stool lunch stand called The Pantry from two elderly ladies. (Former Los Angeles Mayor, Richard Riordan still owns the Original Pantry in downtown Los Angeles.) When they handed him the bill of sale, they laughed and pointed to two stools behind the counter and said, "They go with the place - you're going to need them." Bob told the ladies, "I won't need them. I don't intend to sit down. I won't have the time." That was the beginning. (A few years earlier and less than ten miles away, another mustachioed entrepreneur sold his Moon roadster to pay for the sound on a cartoon . . . Walt Disney.)

Sixteen hours a day, seven days a week, as cook, waiter, and dishwasher, this was the initial return for his investment. But there was more—an opportunity to put into effect his philosophy of restaurant operation, to serve the best food at reasonable prices and in an immaculate restaurant, with courtesy and hospitality..

His first customers were Porter Kelly, Les Lebow, and Gas House Riley.

In February of 1937, some musicians from the Harry Lewis Dance Band (later to become the Chuck Foster Orchestra), then playing at the Biltmore Hotel in Los Angeles, came in for their usual late night snack. The bass player, "Stew" Strange, asked for something different. Bob, in his employee handbook, describes the concoction: "I split the regular hamburger bun through the middle twice instead of once. Between each slice I placed a grilled hamburger patty, mayonnaise, lettuce, cheese, salt, and a special relish, half wrapped it in tissue and put it in a bag." It caught on, even though the musicians were more amused than Bob thought necessary. Soon others were asking for 'the special.'" He knew he had the start of something big. The special had to have a name, and it came about in a most unusual way. A chubby 6-year-old named Richard Woodruff, who lived a few doors away at 812 East Colorado, would sweep up and do little odd jobs for Bob in exchange for the special". Always dressed in loose long trousers held up by a pair of sagging suspenders, Richard was not thin. One time Bob momentarily forgot the young man's name when calling out to him to sweep out the diner. He said, "Hey, Big Boy..." and something clicked

. . . Big Boy. And a name for the special was born: Big Boy, the Original Double Deck Hamburger.

Richard Woodruff, some 15 years later, worked as a cook at Bob's No.1 Drive-In. After Richard's death in 1986, his brother, Glenn, said Richard had a special relationship with Wian. "After Wian became famous, he would come and see my brother, give him an allowance to keep him out of trouble, because we kind of came from a broken family. He even offered to send him to college. My brother could go into any Bob's Big Bob Restaurant and sign his name and eat." No one else, regardless of station or stature, was given this privilege.

Bennie Woshem, who later became a Warner Bros. and Walt Disney cartoonist, designed the original Big Boy without the hamburger. Shortly after, he added the double deck cheeseburger

to Big Boy's right hand. Bennie was an old friend of Bob's and a former coworker at White Log Cabin Coffee Shops.

Many refinements to the Big Boy logo took place over the years. Paper supplier Ken Bird, a good friend of Bob and his dad, had his company's artist do an improved design as a means of getting a big order for their three-color glassine bag in which the Big Boy was served. Manfred Bernhard also assisted in the design of the older standing Big Boy figure. Advertising practitioners, menu suppliers, and others contributed subtle changes. The running Big Boy logo was a compromise.

Dave Bennett, a Frisch franchisee in Toledo, and I later sold Bob Wian and Jack Maier, Frisch's top man in Cincinnati, Ohio, on a common Big Boy design: a running, checkered-pants Big Boy character. We did away with blue-striped pants with cap figure to the more animated running boy with checkered overalls and no cap. Bob's, of course, kept the standing Big Boy for most of their marketing efforts.

Bob, when interviewed in 1972, told a journalist:

"I took a hamburger sauce and a hamburger from a place I had worked, Sternbergers; a system from another place; the pie a la mode and the milk shake from another, and that's the whole Big Boy formula. The system came from the White Log Cabin Coffee Shops, the food from the Rite Spot, the pancake batter from White Log. The pie a la mode wasn't served with a scoop of ice cream that would drip all over the place, but with a slab.... That's the whole deal. All the kids were going to Tom Croupiers for them. Shakes and pie alamode—they were going to Sternbergers for their hamburger, and the White Log Cabins were making all the money. Pie alamode was a tremendous seller if the pies were good. They had to be. I used to make that damn dough by hand. I'm not kidding you, it was tough.""

Bob's grandmother on his father's side baked the pies in the kitchen of her apartment for the first six months. But the demand was so great that Bob bought a bakery. He would go to work at 3:00 in the morning and bake the pies.

"All those pies, cherry, berry, apple, fresh baked. Used to wheel them in at 11:00 every morning and, man, they were a superb cut of pie. Never forget it. I'd fill up the back end of my Chevy, take them and put them in the case. They were so hot that when I cut into them, the glass case would steam up. That was the whole deal. I'd be out of pies by 4:00 in the afternoon. You're thinking, on purpose. Well, not really. We just couldn't bake enough. They were so super good; you know...the real old-fashioned pie with sugar on the top. God, they were pretty.

"We had this little place, and next to it was a wine shop. I can't remember the landlord's name, but my rent was $20 a month. I always knew when the rent was due, because I'd look down the street and see him coming for his money. So the winery went broke and was vacant. I said to the landlord, I'll give you $25 for the place next door. He said, 'You've got a deal,' so I gave him the $25 and tore the place down, because now I was going to make a drive-in out of it; so I made the drive-in and put decomposed granite on the lot, and in about a month I got the joint all finished, and the guy came down the street for the rent, and I see him...he's walking, not on my side of the street, but on the other side. I think, What the hell is he doing on the other side of the street? Finally, he says, 'Where's the wine shop?' I said, I tore it down. He said, You just can't do that. I said, Why can't I do it? I've lowered your taxes, and you're getting the same rent. Well, I thought he was going to have a fit. You know, I was just 21 at the time. I didn't understand. Anyway, he said, 'You just can't do that;

you can't tear my building down; you owe me.' I said, 'Owe you what?' He shuffled his feet a couple of times, raised his eyes looking straight at me and said, $4,500. I said, 'I'll pay it. He said, How are you going to pay $4,500? I said, $45 down and so much a month. And he almost had a fit. He walked away, stopped, turned around still angry and frustrated, and said, 'Okay.'

"So next door a guy's got a nursery with a lath house [greenhouse]. Next thing that happened, a kid comes barreling through the drive-in in his hot rod one evening, loses his brakes and goes right through the lath house...busts it all up. Pots, plants, flowers, small trees, fertilizer, wood lath all over the place. So the guy comes over the next morning, and was he mad. I thought he was going to have a heart attack. He said, Boy, one of your customers went through my lath house last night...broke up all my pots and plants. I said, That's not my fault; you should have a fence over there. The guy just broke up the place before somebody else helped himself. He said, Maybe, but I know I'm out of business. I don't have money to rebuild that lath house. Take a little responsibility for your customers.

14

Show some respect. So, I said, I'll buy the whole place. How much do you want? You'll buy it? he asked. I said, Yup, what do you want? He said, $7,500 for the works. That's for 100 feet on Colorado Boulevard. We made the deal, and I gave the guy $200 down.

"So now we're getting really big. Anyway, I expanded the drive-in then the guy who lived in the little house in the back has a two-year-old daughter, and the headlights from the drive-in customers are going in the windows, and one morning he comes in and said, 'I can't stand the noise. I can't stand the lights, my kid can't sleep. I told the City, but nobody seems to want to do anything about it. I said, 'Gee, that's a shame. Why can't

you sell it?'

"He says, I can't sell it with all the noise and commotion going on around here all night. I said, 'What do you want for it?' He said, $3,500. I said, I'll buy it. So now I've got 400 feet of frontage on Colorado Boulevard and the whole thing is starting to build up. And that's the way the whole damn thing started."

The enthusiasm during this interview, relating something that happened 40 years before, was typical of Bob. He was the magnificent optimist.

Some thought that Bob named his restaurant after the "Original Pantry" in downtown Los Angeles that opened in 1924 and is still thriving. Not true . . . the little stand he purchased from the old ladies was called "The Pantry"

His first drive-in was a barnburner. It opened at 5:00 P.M. and was full until at least 10 P.M. Traffic was a real problem as the line-up of cars along the curb would begin about 4:30, and by 5:00 there were more cars in line than spaces in the drive-in. Colorado Boulevard was a two-lane major thoroughfare connecting Glendale and Pasadena, and the police would assist the restaurant customers by keeping the parking lane alongside the curb clear for the line-up. On one occasion, a driver with Iowa license plates found himself in the line, not realizing what it was for. When he got to the front, another officer waved him in and the lot attendant directed him into a space. When the car hop approached the driver to take his order, "May I help you, sir?", the driver finally got the message and shouted, "I don't want any of your stupid food; I'm just trying to get to Pasadena. I want to see the Rose Bowl before it gets dark." The carhop, embarrassed, apologized. The driver, cooling off a little, asked, "Can you make me a hamburger to take with me?" He got his Big Boy and was last seen going east on Colorado Boulevard.

From the Los Angeles Times, November 2, 1993: "Big Mac is boning up for a home deliv-

Bob Wian, 1936...the start of something Big...Boy

ery attack. So are Kentucky Fried Chicken, Subway and El Polo Loco. As fast as you can phone or fax your request, these familiar fast-food names are starting to deliver—to the home or the office.""

In 1949 Bob introduced home delivery using little Crosley cars; the service was very successful. Managed by a brother-in-law, Dick Weis, the food was prepared at Bob's No.1 Coffee Shop and loaded into the tiny white cars with the Big Boy insignia painted on the sides. Problems arose with the tremendous response to the delivery idea, as it was taxing the restaurant proper. The preparation was then moved to separate cooking facilities a couple of blocks away, but even then they had problems. Too many cooks were being taken out of the restaurant to please Bob. He knew that a poor morale situation was being created, as the cooks were not in the restaurants. They wanted to be where the action was, keep in touch with the public, fellow cooks, carhops, waitresses and cashiers, especially the carhops, waitresses and cashiers. What to do? He shut it down.

From the archives 1936 to 1942

WAITRESSES & CARHOPS

Drive-ins in the late 30's, 40's, 50's and 60's were the place to be seen if you were on the make, to show off a beautiful car or, lastly, to eat. Bob's was the most popular of all the Los Angeles drive-ins. There were also Herbert's, Carpenter's, Tiny Naylor's, Henry's, Dolores', Van de Kamp's, Simon's, and Robert's. Without a doubt the carhops (attendants) were something to see, watch, and envy. They were great looking, all had good figures to better fit into their uniforms, and they could really move. They had to be fast, often running from counter to car during most of their shift. Bob's was the first to pay the carhops and allow them to keep all of their tips. They ran all the way to the bank, too. Some other drive-ins not only didn't pay carhops by the hour, but also took some of the tip money. Read Jim Heimann's book "CAR HOPS and CURB SERVICE" if you want to learn everything worth knowing about drive-in restaurants.

Obviously, Bob's was the place to be if you wanted to be a carhop. All the customers you could possibly handle meant more tips in a clean, wholesome atmosphere, plus generous customers, many of them movie stars who regularly ate outside in their cars for privacy.

It was not unusual for the girls to work 10 years or more as a carhop -Christine Heater worked 25 years, Esther Chrostowski 15. With seniority you got the best stations. At the Toluca Lake drive-in in Burbank (#6), there were 60 stalls. The station furthest away had six stalls. The closest also had six stalls directly in front of the window or counter from which the food was picked up and placed on the trays to be taken to the car. The No.1 girl, therefore, walked not more than 20 feet to her customers, while the new girl on the block, like Donna Sekyra, ran at least 60 feet each way from counter to car.

Irene Wright, a Joan Crawford look-a-like who didn't know how to frown, was for years the No.1 girl at Toluca Lake. Auburn hair, beautiful skin, teeth, and figure, Irene was constantly pursued by the young and not-so-young men about town. Because of her expertise and short walk to her customers, Irene looked as camera-ready at the end of her shift as the rest of the girls did at the start of theirs.

Hopping cars was more glamorous and attracted the athletic young women, but the waitresses inside the coffee shops were the ones who set the standard for service. They wore simple uniforms: full black skirt, white short-sleeve blouse (Ship 'n Shore), white apron, and white flats with nylon stockings. No beehive hairdo, no long fingernails, no strong perfume, no excessive avoirdupois, but everything else. Attractive, clean, great teeth, quick, pleasant but not patronizing. Bob's waitresses were quite simply the very best. Because the waitresses' physical demands were less than the carhops', good waitresses were encouraged to stay as long as they wished. It was not unusual for a waitress to work 20 to 30 years. June Forte, Sandy Hallock, Carol Mayes, Betty Fagan, Jerry Ogg. Then came superstars like Pat Dewhurst and Bonnie Tuesburg and there were many many more. When researching the material for this story, I went into a Bob's in Glendale and the waitress was Betty Santoro—

a great looking girl with the same attitude and appearance that I knew 30 years before. They were special. Many, like the late Betty Fagan, would head up task forces all over the country to help new franchisees; some would become hostess managers; still others would marry the boss. Those who stayed continuously for a long period of time also left Bob's with pension trust funds in excess of several hundred thousand dollars..

All of the great waitresses at Bob's were trained or influenced by Big Boy veteran Florence Hansen (no relation), who served the organization for 35 years. If there was a formula on the Big Boy approach to service personnel, it was hiring people who liked people, never brought problems to the job, were ambitious to be in a dynamic company or simply to be helping hungry customers enjoy a good meal without distractions, and were people with-

DAY PERSONNEL
Front Row — Left to Right: Mary Anderson, Carma Toole, Faye Powell, Rowena Norton, Dorothy Job, Delores Sinclair, Joannie Schultz.
Middle Row — Left to Right: Retha McCue, Lillian Size, Peggy Walker, Tess Kalinowski, Mary Whitaker, Elizabeth Allen, Betty Galbreath, Ramona Lake, Marilyn Schmidt, Janet Moore, Patricia Maxwell, Louise Calderon, Glenn Martin, Executive Manager.
Back Row — Left to Right: Martin Zimmermann, Frank Nyerges, Bernard Hughes, Dave Halliwell, Edward Floyd, Huey Hughes, Carl Moeschler, Elmer Tuesburg, Day Manager, Coffee Shop, Robert McCallum, Day Manager, Drive-In, William Manning.

NIGHT PERSONNEL
Front Row — Left to Right: Diane Reid, Gladys De Roos, Dorothy Makray, Sarah Bradford, Marilyn Howey, Gloria Maffia, Margaret Lewis, Louise Harrison, Dorothy Fuller, Nancy Glenn.
Middle Row — Left to Right: James Gaudino, Donald Fagan, Night Manager, Drive-In, Bruce McCormick, Grayce Fowler, Beverly Leineke, Mary Ferguson, Margaret Wilson, Shirley Snead, Jeane Dennewitz, Ronald Milch, Germida Bonton, Richard Holman, Night Mgr., Coffee Shop.
Back Row — Left to Right: William Manning, Sam Thaw, Edward Campbell, Henry Cieminski, Walter Painter, Robert Ingham, Henry Helpingstine, Richard Harper, Robert Kahley, John Nolan, Joe Vazquez, William Roberts.

out an "attitude". The customers were congenial and generous. They expected the best and got it. The waitresses were happy, friendly people just waiting to serve you the best food in town. Bob's liked to think that, "BEHIND EVERY BIG BOY THERE'S A HAPPY SMILING FACE."

I spent a couple of weeks at the Harvard Business School in 1966 and learned from two professors in particular, that the bottom line is God. Service seldom mentioned, quality never. This was at the time the Japanese were taking no prisoners in the automobile industry selling quality, economy of operation, and price. Both teachers let the class know that they were consultants to two of Detroit's biggest.

One of the fellows was from Pasadena, California. My goodness, all he had to do was go to Bob's Big Boy on Colorado Blvd. to learn something about quality, service, price and respect for the customer.

The Harvard folks didn't ask me to stick around so the only thing I really learned was that arrogance in relation to the consumer is bad business. By the way, during one of the cocktail hours I walked over to Harvard's football stadium. It was secured . . . with Yale locks. I wonder how long it took the professors to fess up to clients that they were asleep in class.

DAY PERSONNEL
Front Row — Left to Right: Janice Kuzia, Betty Stratton, Marilyn Warner, Donna Collins, Florence Weeks, Fern Austin, Jean Day, Patricia Thomson, Hella Perea.
Middle Row — Left to Right: James Dougherty, Mgr. Drive-In, Florence Hansen, Mary Pease, Roxana Annis, Jeanine Male, Janice Needlman, Patricia Brown, Bettye Holland, Darlene MacDonald, Maria Lob, Barbara Hensley, Leora Reinhart, Rose Mestyanek, Marilyn Mattox, Robert Eakin, Executive Mgr.
Back Row — Left to Right: Mauro Martinez, Edward Malatia, William Armstrong, Le Roy Schill, George Latsko, John Gieske, Paul Soltis, Leo Zukoski, Lyle Boyd, Mgr. Coffee Shop, Franklin Stieringer.

NIGHT SHIFT
Front Row — Left to Right: Dorothy Smith, Emma Pironti, Eunice Jones, Margaret Spain, Ruby Price, Francis Ruiz, Joy Rusk, Patricia Lewsadder, Judy Gogal.
Middle Row — Left to Right: William Walker, Mgr. Coffee Shop, Dorothy Melton, Doris Gallant, Judy Quinn, Betty Lee, Clarese Bures, Andra Kee, Merle Palm, William Simone, Mgr. Drive-In.
Back Row — Left to Right: Dewey Stoops, Manuel de la Torre, Clifford Wilson, Norman Deering, H. A. Martin, Philip Munson, Harry Bower, Tom Vande Lune, Howard O'Grady, Stewart Andrews, Rexford Call.

DAY PERSONNEL
Front Row — Left to Right: Lois Youngflesh, Eva Christensen, Sophie Kolmsee, Eula Odstreil, Grace Halliwell, Lu Ella Peralta, Rachel Vejar, Martha Jones, Dorothy Brace, Willa Mae Machen, Pat DePew, Laurel Swanson, Phillipp Schmidt, Day Manager.
Back Row — Left to Right: David Barnett, Robert Millar, Dale Dungan, Assistant Day Manager, Harry Meer, Thomas Plankenhorn, Thomas Hanshaw.

NIGHT PERSONNEL
Front Row — Left to Right: Robert Glassett, Manager, Florine Oaks, Belle Kahley, Mavis Heyer, Margaretta Olsen, Bette Shaffner, Karen Braley, Louise Osborne, Lorraine Swan.
Back Row — Left to Right: Benjamin DeGeneres, Charles Metcalf, Don Schumacher, Donald Hoard, Richard Ingham, Assistant Night Manager, James Medley, Flaviano Montoya.

DAY PERSONNEL
Front Row — Left to Right: Betty Wait, Mary McKeon, Joan Hertzler, Betty Devig, Mary Pennington, Patsy Eldredge, Alice Stephens.
Middle Row — Left to Right: Betty Bennett, De Wayn Meek, Patricia Barrows, Nancy McCormick, Nancy Khougaz, Shirley Watts, Mary Boncyk, Catherine Swieda, Donna Olson, Frances Wagner, Gilford LeFrancois, Day Manager, Drive-In, Donald Seltzer.
Back Row — Left to Right: Johanne Lamers, Harry Matthews, Day Manager, Coffee Shop, Carl Mahlstedt, Ronald Inman, Frederick Cuthbert, Richard Griffin, Maurice DeForge, Rayburn Surrett, C. D. Grogan.

NIGHT PERSONNEL
Front Row — Left to Right: Geraldine Kline, Betty Hamlin, Lila Williams, Annette Cloos, Peggy Dugas, Nola Bradford, Loretta Morrow, Lynn Mercier, Betty North, Joann Kent, Neoma Martens.
Middle Row — Left to Right: Edward Glassett, Executive Manager, Elsie Raner, Jeanell Wood, Joyce Phelps, Marilyn Caplette, Frances Spencer, Jerri Rebullosa, Betty Hayn, June Hefele, Mark Depew, Night Manager, Drive-In.
Back Row — Left to Right: Hiram Peachy, Robert Callaway, Night Manager, Coffee Shop, Willard Hibbler, Harlyn Prouty, Gene Collins, William Farris, Donald Jones, Donald Harris, Robert Kingsbury, James Dillon, Peter Perrucci.

DAY PERSONNEL
Front Row — Left to Right: Yvonne Vernor, Peggy Honea, Doris Smith, Betty Cozzens, Jea Panda, Janice Morgan, Georgia Schill, Norman Spiegelberg, Day Mgr.
Back Row — Left to Right: James Christenson, James Annis, David Burkhart, Asst. Da Mgr., George Campbell, Albert Kruer.

NIGHT PERSONNEL
Front Row — Left to Right: Evelyn Ferrara, Marion Pappas, Betty Nielsen, Shirley Morter Ruth Fagan, Jacqueline Crowther, Alice Rockwood, Jean Gilmore, Merrillyn Tiedemann
Back Row — Left to Right: Roger Clark, Asst. Night Mgr., John Mead, Luis Carrillo, Clar Raner, William Marsh, Eutimio Morales, A. Bruce Breyfogle, Mgr.

DAY PERSONNEL
Front Row — Left to Right: Lora Sullivan, Shirley Leisure, Betty Ramseyer Jonita Smith, Margaret Rodriquez Johanna McCabe.
Middle Row — Left to Right: William Freeman, Day Mgr., Eleanor Johnston, Marie Daoust, Genevieve Morris, Zella Mulkey, Marilyn Peterson, Wayne Rich.
Back Row — Left to Right: Jack Twiss, Billy Brookshire, Buddy Quine, Carl Thornton, Asst. Day Mgr., Larry Stump, Patrick Sewnig.

NIGHT PERSONNEL
Front Row — Left to Right: Oletamae Dever, Joyce Tremel, Thelma Patskan, Joan Callaway, Selma Story.
Middle Row — Left to Right: Milton Spencer, Mgr., John Gregory, Betty Opilowsky, Vyla Riner, Bryce Adcock, Asst. Mgr.
Back Row — Left to Right: Fred Gilbertson, Edwin Brann, Henry Lemons, Elton McEldowney Jerry La Rue, John Caputo.

DAY PERSONNEL
Front Row — Left to Right: Dorothy Crain, Belva Kirkpatrick, Jeraldine Turner, Sharon Shepherd, Patricia Dunphy, Mary Tidwell, Mary Lorenzen, Marie Nicassio, Barbara Cook, Ila Mason, June Wight.
Back Row — Left to Right: Varoujian Derderian, Orville Spence, Joe Tidwell, Robert Raner, Day Mgr., Herbert Sutton, Asst. Day Mgr., Charles Powell, Robert Drining.

NIGHT PERSONNEL
Front Row — Left to Right: Vineta Jarrett, Sandra Gasaway, Barbara Thomas, Lavella Ingham Julia Campbell, Jacqueline Kurtz, Robin Ingram, Betty Helm.
Back Row — Left to Right: Roland Talbot, Casimiro Perez, Clarence Vassey, Richard Panda Asst. Night Mgr., Virgil Hammond, David Densmore, Richard Adams.
Not Shown: Hermann Weber, Mgr.

CUSTOMERS

Requests by film and TV people to shoot inside the restaurants were frequent but never granted. We would, however, let them use an isolated part of the drive-in if they finished before the 11:00 a.m. opening. Don't misunderstand, Bob did not discourage shows like "Queen for a Day" rolling a woman on a bed the mile from NBC to have breakfast in bed at Bobs Drive-In, or a "Truth or Consequences" stunt starring the worlds largest Big Boy Hamburger. Even Bob was willing to be featured on "You Bet Your Life" with Groucho Marx. He was terrific, as was Groucho. Only a two or three-minute drive from Warner Bros. and Universal studios, NBC, Columbia Ranch, and Lakeside Golf Club, Bob's Drive-In was not only a convenience but also a requisite for busy movie industry types wanting to eat quickly and stay in the car.

Customers were not allowed to leave their cars except to use the restroom. This rule was strictly enforced by at least two lot attendants during the busy hours, which was most of the time. Trying to keep younger romantics from seeing an old flame up close and personal was not as difficult as one might imagine. Simply put, if the customers didn't follow the rules, they were eighty-sixed, and because Bob's was the place to be, enforcement was not too difficult. Customers seldom became ornery because alcohol and drug problems were extremely rare in those days.

It was a time, however, when NBC's "Saturday Night Live" regulars (Chevy Chase, John Belushi, Dan Aykroyd) and "The Tonight Show's" Johnny Carson made jokes about drug use which, in my opinion, was a major reason drugs became acceptable to millions of gullible yuppies, and now their children. Some of the fools are still laughing, but many others laughed their last laugh a long time ago. It was also a time when Richard Pryor, Whoopie Goldberg, and later Eddie Murphy, Bette Midler, George Carlin and Dennis Miller copied the Lenny Bruce foul mouth routine to further their careers. They had enough talent to get by without the F word but didn't know it. Bruce, with his marginal comedic talent, had no choice but to do what he did. Has anyone ever complained that there wasn't enough foul language in a comedian's act, a TV show, or a motion picture?

Movie stars who were regulars at the Toluca Lake and Burbank drive-ins would fill a theater: Bob Hope, Debbie Reynolds, Jonathan Winters, Dana Andrews, Glendale's Alexis Smith, Craig Stevens, and Mickey Rooney, the performing arts' most gifted entertainer. Bob Hope, not always alone, and an investor in Big Boy Franchises Inc. ($100,000), was a regular at the Bob's Drive-In in Burbank. It was off the beaten path on San Fernando Road, affording privacy, although other customers rarely bothered Bob's celebrity status. Occasionally, he would try out a joke on me. When he remarked about his new 4-door

Jerry Colonna, Bob Wian, Bob Hope, Pat O'Brien

Cadillac with the fins, Hope said, "Yeah, it's about the size of a Texas phone booth." I countered that it was more like a bachelor's apartment. He didn't write it down.

Another well-known contributor to Bob's Big Boy Drive-Ins' popularity was George Barris, the premier custom car builder for the motion picture industry, whose styling genius was copied by body shops catering to custom car buffs. Bob's Big Boy in Toluca Lake was the place to "show off" gorgeous recreations—lowered, twin pipes, twenty coats of lacquer—WOW.

Rock Hudson, a young contract player at Universal, regularly ate Sunday morning breakfast at the Toluca Lake drive-in. He always parked at the far end of the lot, but in every case he used the restroom at the front of the lot. He always looked over, but never spoke.

One Sunday, Susan Ball, another Universal contract player, came in with Anthony Quinn, parking a couple of feet from where I stood. Susan, a stunning brunette, was a regular at Bob's, and being seen with a major star like Quinn was a real coup. Quinn, driving a convertible with the top down, did not relish the "Looky-Loos" in the adjoining stalls. In addition, he was not thrilled by my remarks when it was obvious that Susan had given a lot more to Quinn than directions to Bob's Big Boy. When Susan went to powder her nose, I reminded Quinn that Susan was just a kid and shouldn't be taken advantage of. If Quinn's looks could kill, the funeral would have been the following Tuesday. I thought I'd walk over to Hudson, who knew Susan (they were on the same lot), and ask him to give her a little protection from the big bad wolf. But Rock, without a stunt man, would have been in real trouble. Susan did go on to make some features, married, but died much too young, as did her husband, Richard "Big Valley" Long.

There were all kinds of restaurants in the area. It wasn't as if Bob's was the only place around or had the best waitresses and prettiest carhops. It was simply that they had the best total combination of food, service, and prices. Bob Wian demanded perfection and got it by setting standards so high that everyone wanted to be part of Bob's Big Boy, the best food service company in the country.

Burt Lancaster   Bob Wian

A couple of young guys who made it!

Bob's had the best customers in the world, and not just the famous ones. True, they didn't have much to complain about, which made Bob's a very pleasant place to eat. The action was contagious from inside and out. All of the Big Boy Coffee Shops were built as close to the street as legal, with massive glass windows. Driving or walking by practically put you inside the restaurant. It was an entertainment, almost like a stage play with all the action, color, and costumes. From the outside, a silent movie. Inside, the talkies.

Another reason for the customers' good will was the fact that anything that was not prepared exactly as described on the menu was cheerfully exchanged, and never did a waitress "agree to agree", walk away, and frown later. She and the cooks didn't get their feelings hurt, because meeting the menu description gave both of them the chance to please the customer, and a significant amount of the waitress' income was tips. Bob felt that the customers did him a favor by their patronage, and he never forgot it.

[BOB] "Do you know the greasy spoon type of joint years ago the average person had to eat in? It was crummy. All I did was clean it up and serve better food, nicer. Once you get something thrown in your face, you decide that you're going to do it a little bit differently in relation to service of food to the middle class person. They eat better now than the successful and wealthy did then, and they get better service, because it's done with more sincerity. But there was a renaissance in this business, and it happened in the early 1930's when the average person didn't have a place like McDonald's to go to where they thank you for serving yourself. So all I did was to sit them down at a table and thank them for coming and served them at the same time. A sociological change was taking place. It goes back to the great coal miner union guy, John L. Lewis. That was when the change started to take place that the average working man was soon going to require something better than was being served, which was slop, cold coffee, dirty cups, unsanitary restaurant conditions. This was the part of the renaissance that started the Big Boy. Believe it or not, it's fundamental. I took from the people a philosophy and awareness of what the public wanted...I was also aware of the trend that was going to take place, and tried to put it into a package that would be lasting...and brought in my own points of view relative to the help. There was no book written on that. But you would assume that when the working man would expect something better, he wasn't going to expect only better from the place he dined in, but he was going to expect something better from the people he worked for, so there was a complete refining of all of these elements, and it's all there today. Actually, it was a renaissance in the food service industry for the middle class."

LIKE FATHER, LIKE SON

[BOB]   "My dad never forgot that I was the boss, and I never
forgot that I was his son. My dad was a great man, a great man."

Robert E. "Pappy" Wian died from cerebral hemorrhage complications in 1948. He was 57. The 104-car funeral procession was at the time the largest in the history of Glendale, California's, famous Forest Lawn Memorial Park. The cars detoured to drive by Bob's Big Boy, Home of the Original Double-Decked Hamburger, the enterprise to which he was such an important contributor.

In Philadelphia, Bob's dad, a jeweler, later worked for Abbott Dairies selling ice cream. On weekends he would go around the neighborhood demonstrating Wearever Aluminum. He would put on a big dinner and got to be quite a cook. In 1925, when Bob was 11, Pappy got the money together, and the family took the train out to California. Pappy contacted an old friend in the furniture business. He later started the Jewel Furniture Company, which was very successful, creating custom-made draperies and furniture for apartment house complexes. He built a big Spanish three-story house with balconies and verandas, where he and wife Cora (Trudel) were well known for their hospitality. Both liked playing cards, and always had something going on with their many friends from the entertainment business. Bob's sister Dottie said,

"Bob was very much like his dad. In fact, Daddy was really the
business head in the family, but in the depression in 1929 and the early

30's Daddy lost everything. He was selling beer by the carload for Maier Brewing Company when he threw in with Bob in 1936. He took care of the buying and was around to soft-shoe Bob's big drives. Bob needed balance at the time, and he learned a lot from his father, who worked with Bob as purchasing agent and confidante until Pappy's stroke in 1948.

"At first, Bob would grind the meat, cook the Big Boys, walk around to the customer and serve them, but business was so good that Daddy took over the meat grinding. There was a lot of suspicion in those days about meat, so all of the hamburger patties were ground fresh every day. He would stand there all day grinding meat and slicing cheese."

Mayor Bob Wian and Glendale City Officials

Dottie said that her parents, of German-French-Austrian ancestry, were Presbyterians in Philadelphia but Methodists in Glendale. She said that her parents took the children to church from infancy to late teens, but never attended with them.

Dottie also recalled, "Bob was a ham, a leader, he was always in variety shows, had a lot of musical lessons and all kinds of musical instruments, never doing too well on any of them, but he was always very popular with the teachers, even though scholastically he was just average. He worked in the high school cafeteria sometimes, for his dad in the furniture store, and on Saturdays at Arrowhead Water. He wasn't really outstanding at anything, but everybody liked him; he was a personality, with a lot of ambition, which he got from his dad. They both liked to entertain, liked cards, liked people."

Bob said, regarding those high school years, "I guess I forged as many blue slips as anyone in high school."

28

There were only 297 students in Bob Wian's graduating class at Glendale High School in 1933. But Bob was so popular that everybody who ever went to Glendale High later claimed they went to school with him. You would think there must have been thousands in his senior class. This "myth information" gave some people the idea that Bob was much younger or much older than he actually was. After all, when someone who was 40 when Bob was 50, or vice versa, said they went to school with Bob, well. One thing sure, Bob never denied he went to school with anybody. He was flattered, and that was what made Bob the special and ingratiating personality he was. Nowadays, they call it charisma; back then they called people like Bob "a great guy".

Bob Wian   Nancy Reagan,   *"House Guests"*   Ronald Reagan   June Wian

Some of Bob's Executive Staff resented it when some when local businesses used the name "Bob" in their signage. They felt that Bob had an exclusive right to use the name, and they were serious. No one ever heard Bob complain. And no one called Bob Wian "Mr. Wian" more than once. The first time was the last. Without being prompted, everybody knew it was perfectly all right to call this highly-respected, accomplished, generous, inventive, wealthy, ex-fry cook, Bob. Don't be misled. Bob was not a "Good 'ole Bob" kind of guy when something was not quite kosher. Many a time, when he was dining in some of the finest restaurants in the country, those in charge felt his displeasure when service or quality was not in keeping with the environment and the prices. On the other hand, when things were right, he let management, particularly the chef and his staff know that their efforts were appreciated, and the gratuity reflected his feelings.

Bob never played the "Do you know who I am?" routine. They knew who he was, this hamburger guy from California. When Bob walked into a room, everything stopped, from Mama Leone's to Luchows, Trader Vic's in New York, Brennan's and Antoine's in New Orleans, Ernie's in San Francisco, Don the Beachcomber in Hollywood, the Pump Room in Chicago, Chasen's in Los Angeles, London Chop House in Detroit, to the great hot dog places in New York and downtown Detroit. Bob was someone to be catered to. Bob, when speaking of his company, always said, "We should be a good company to do business with." He practiced it and expected others to do the same.

In the 30's and 40's, Glendale, California, was famous for many things: Forest Lawn Memorial Park, award-winning floats in the Tournament of Roses Parade, baseball's Babe Herman and Casey Stengel, football's Frankie Albert, Indianapolis car builder Al J. Watson, boxer lightweight champion boxer Jimmy McLarnin, and others who were famous in their own right. But Bob Wian was truly the boy wonder. He made Glendale even more famous.

Frank Kurtis, of Kurtis Kraft Automobile fame, made a car for Bob—a whole car. In 1952 ('53 model) Bob also had the first Corvette in Southern California, white with red leather upholstery. He owned a race horse, was an avid fisherman from his 27-foot Hunter Cruiser; and regularly patronized Glendale's Grand Central Airport (the airport location in the movie Casablanca) for the fun and excitement of flying..

During World War II, Grand Central was the headquarters for what was called "The Flying Sergeants." These were a group of Army enlisted men trained in P-38's, built by Burbank-based Lockheed, specifically for low-level strafing missions against Rommel's tank corps in North Africa. Carol Shelby, world renowned race car driver, designer (Cobra Le Mans, Monte Carlo), and innovator, was an instructor of Flying Sergeants at Randolf Field in Texas. Bob, along with best friend Joe Scalzo, adopted the group, as he did many others during the war. Bob had tried to enlist in the Army and the Merchant Marine during World War II, but was turned down due to a hernia and the fact that he was born with one kidney. He was also married and a father at the time. During Vietnam, Bob asked to be allowed to go to Vietnam unannounced to serve Big Boys to the troops, but the State Department did not embrace the idea and nothing came of it.

These extracurricular activities and others took their toll, and at 27 years of age he developed a bleeding ulcer that almost took his life. On his doctor's recommendation, he was told to drink Port wine to help fortify his anemic condition due to loss of blood. The doctor also prescribed that he occasionally put his feet up on his desk, lean back and smoke a cigarette. Relax. Bob took the advice and then some. From then on, Bob as a part-time but serious drinker and a full-time smoker of Camel cigarettes.

The premature death of Pappy Wian may have had more influence on Bob's lifestyle than generally realized. Even though he outlived his father by almost thirty years, there was more than one close call for Bob. In his twenties, bleeding ulcers; kidney trouble in his thirties; and internal problems of another nature in his forties. Still, in his fifties, Bob refused to have much needed dental work performed, because he felt the expense would not be justified for such, he thought, a short period of time. Mickey Mantle syndrome because of his dad and his son Bobby's serious illnesses? Maybe. He did, however, have the dental work done.

Bob's father was prominent in community affairs in Philadelphia, but Bob was to become the consummate activist in Glendale, California. Bob was recognized as an accomplished extemporaneous public speaker, but in later years he begged off speaking in formal situations. However, he was always promoting his city, his restaurants, and his image. He was an active member of the Lion's Club, 20-30 Club, and Junior Chamber of Commerce. Bob at one time was California's and Glendale's youngest mayor, 1945-46.

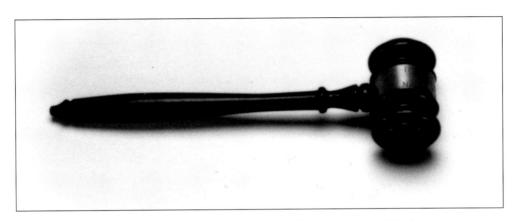

Presented to His Honor, The Mayor. 1946

Stork Club New York City: Bob Wian, John Elias, Casey Stengel, Edna Stengel

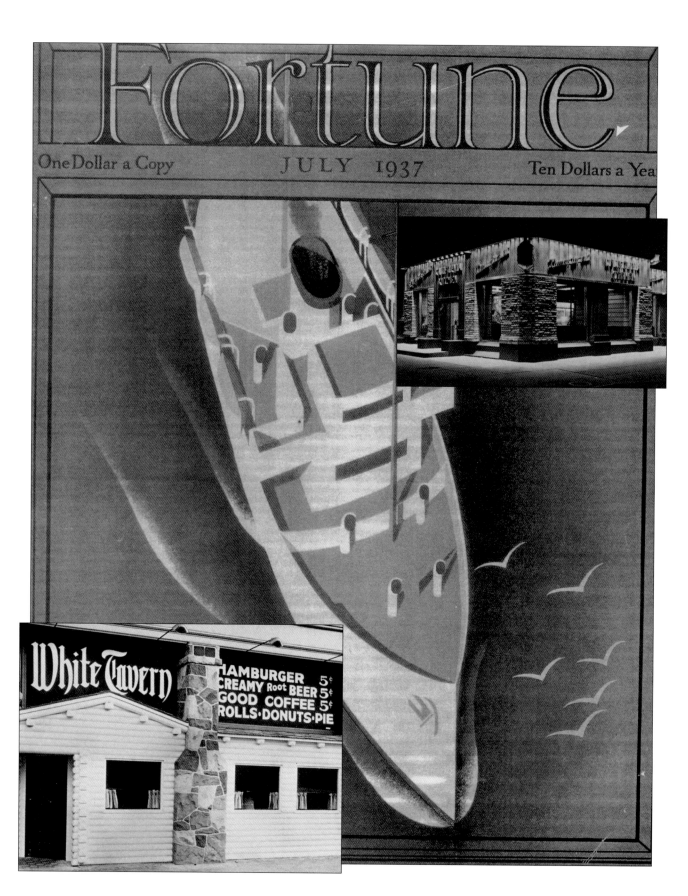

INNOVATORS

Famous names in American commerce include entrepreneurs J. C. Penney, Sam Walton, Henry Ford, and Marshall Field. But in the food service business, Bob Wian stands head and shoulders above the rest.

Bob Wian was destined to be an innovator-entrepreneur in the service or entertainment business. Even in high school he was always "out among 'em with a million ideas and no place to use them. He had to start some place, and that happened at the White Log Coffee Shop at 2nd and Broadway in Los Angeles. He had graduated from Glendale High School in 1931 and coaxed his mother to drive him down to the White Log LA office for an interview. They only interviewed once a week, and there was usually a line of people outside waiting to get in. He got the interview but not the job. So his mother brought him back the following week, and he was hired as a dishwasher on the midnight shift by Los Angeles District Manager Larry Gorvad. At 19, Bob was the manager.

He couldn't have started at a better place. Ken E. Bemis, owner/operator of White Log Coffee Shops, did his part to popularize the word entrepreneur. An investor of note, some of his ventures successful and some not, he certainly knew what to do with an idea. Fortune Magazine in 1937 said that the restaurants Mr. Bemis established on the Pacific Coast were "the best run aggregation of eating houses in the U.S." Other flattering quotes in Fortune included "a creative genius... a shrewd businessman."

White Log Coffee Shops were often confused with White Castle in the Midwest and White Tower along the Atlantic seaboard. In 1935, White Castle sold 36,500,000 hamburgers, 50% of its business. White Tower, with a broader menu, did 35% of its business in hamburgers.

The Fortune article explained the economics of Bemis' business in a striking but simple way. A hardware store operator can have discount sales due to errors in purchasing judgment. The restaurant operator, on the other hand, throws his mistakes in the garbage. And when the restaurateur throws away food, he's throwing away working capital. Fast food restaurants today throw nothing away unless accidentally spoiled or damaged in preparation. That explains why almost anybody can operate a fast food restaurant, particularly if it's a franchise that restricts innovation in the kitchen.

The Fortune article also told of Bemis' son and daughter, Bill and Beverly, who later became famous in their own right as a headline dance team starring on stage and screen in both America and Europe. Bill, who contributed many of the photographs in this chapter, went on to become a Big Boy franchisee in Washington, DC, and Maryland. Always a close associate of Bob, Bill said, "Bob developed the finest organization of its kind ever put together. He built it on loyalty and fairness to everyone that worked for him, and his careful selections of the right people and magnificent training and standards meant there was no place else for them to go—except up."''

Bob, in a letter to Bill Bemis on March 23, 1976, said: "During the forty years with Bob's and Big Boy, your many contributions to the growth and character of the chain and your friendly ways of achieving perfection were most significant. For these I will be ever grateful and I hope you will always consider me as your admiring and very close friend."

After Bob learned the White Log system, he expanded his expertise by working for and associating himself with the most successful operators in the area. The following is from an interview with Bob in 1972, where he describes his relationships and experiences with other restaurateurs.

[BOB] "Lionel Sternberger was the greatest of them all! You know he created the cheeseburger. He came to Pasadena from San Diego in 1916 with his twin brother, Van, to open a fruit stand with his dad. The fruit stand expanded to a fast food restaurant, The Rite Spot. (Another fresh fruit and berry stand became the famous Knott's Berry Farm in Buena Park, California.) After Mr. Sternberger died in 1923, the property was sold, and Lionel and Van opened Henry's, featuring "Chicken in The Rough". Len Dunagan and I worked for Lionel, where Dunagan was my manager. He had hired me away from Bemis' White Log Coffee Shop."

"Lionel was an ingenious food man; a naturally knowledge-able person, he charged a dime for coffee when other people couldn't get a nickel. One time I saw him and his chef making vegetable soup. It was a beautiful soup, and his chef had a 15-gallon stockpot on the stove. Lionel came over, ladled the contents, and as he looked at it, he said to the chef, "Where are the lima beans?" The chef said, "I didn't have any." Lionel said, "Get a hold of that stockpot!" So the chef gets a hold of it, took it over to Lionel, who proceeded to dump the whole 15 gallons right down the drain. He said to the chef, "When I've got a formula, don't you ever put out but what I tell you to do. You could have walked up the street to the market and paid 60¢ for a package of dried lima beans. Don't you ever put out anything unless it's the way I say." The restaurant didn't have soup that day. He did this to impress the chef with the importance of making it right. That's the kind of man he was.

"Lionel also started the Chili Size. I only worked there when somebody wouldn't show up. I'd go over from the Rite Spot and fill in. Sidney Hodemaker was president of Pig Stand. That was what he

brought down from the St. Francis in San Francisco. He was Maitre d' up there. They had 16 Pig Stands in the Los Angeles area. From the Pig Stands came the first really upscale coffee shop, Pig & Whistle at Sunset and Vine.

"Sidney Hodemaker was a great standard bearer in the industry. I worked closely with him because I was on the Board of the National Restaurant Association, along with J. W. Marriott. That was when I first met J. W. Marriott. But Sidney was great, because he would really, truly try to help everybody. He was a student of anything in the food business; he could smell anything that was bad, and instinctively catch the aroma of anything that was good. He was just ingenious; his success testified to that. He started out as a busboy at the St. Francis Hotel in San Francisco and built up this chain of restaurants. First it was Herbert's, and then Hody's. He would know if there was a problem developing; he wouldn't have to trip over it to be able to identify it. He had an instinctive knowledge and an awareness he would share with people. Many of them didn't get the point, but I did."

"Another great operator was Bill Bemis' dad, Ken. Well, he wasn't as great a restaurant man as he was a merchandiser. We had six-cent malts. And he knew how to put a package together. He had a deal with orange juice, two pancakes, one egg, bacon, and coffee for 19 cents. That was a breakfast special.

"Pricing, merchandising, and a system. I got it from him. You

know, a lot of guy's say, 'Okay, I want something like this for dinner,' and they make twice as much as you order and the rest gets thrown away. Well, Bemis Sr. put a system to the food business like White Castle. That's where he got some of his ideas. They served nickel hamburgers in a bag. Bemis was one of the pioneers of systematizing the food business, with a limited menu, and the commissary type of operation, which gives full control of quality and prices.

"There were all sorts of chains springing up, but a lot of them went down the tubes. Then the Brown Derby came along operated by A. J. Sanderson. Bob Cobb, who had worked as manager for Sanderson, eventually bought the Derby, where he invented the Cobb Salad.

"My first drive-in job was the Pig Stand, which I think started in Dallas, Texas. They served a barbecued pork sandwich and had a great big pig out in front. The big men in the food business in those days [30's and 40's] were the Carpenters, Levis, Herberts; they were pioneers of the drive-in business in southern California.

"Charlie Eaton started as a busboy in Kansas City. He came out

here and he worked at Old McGuerin's Toad in the Hole on Hollywood Boulevard. Then he opened a steak house on Wilshire, and a chicken house on La Cienega. Charlie was an ingenious restaurant man. Charlie got his chicken menu from Willard's: mashed potatoes, country gravy, and all the pan-fried chicken you could eat. Super, super meal with fresh peas and, oh God, with biscuits. Their second place was on Los Feliz. My dad used to take us there, and we would eat for about $5.25, all the chicken you could eat. It was a great Sunday outing for all five of us. I was about 14. My sister Dottie was about 12 and Katherine was 10.

"Another great guy I admired in the restaurant business (and I observed them all and went to their places to get ideas for my places) was Carl Anderson down by the Los Angeles Coliseum. I'll tell you a story about Carl. After I had been kind of successful, I'd go fishing in the mountains and stay at a motel, and in the evening I'd sit on the patio. There was a guy next to me in a rocking chair at the place, and he said, 'Where are you from?' I said, 'Los Angeles.' 'What do you do down there?' he said. I said, 'I'm in the restaurant business.' He said, 'I'll be darned, so am I.' It was Carl Anderson, and this was about 1941; that's how I met Carl. We've been dear friends ever since.

"Carl was an instinctive restaurant man, an instinctive food man. He didn't have to measure anything, just...(snap of fingers), you know, they

Car Hops & Curb Service – Jim Heimann

can tell by the aroma how it's going to taste. I'd say Sternberger was and Eaton, even though he wasn't a chef; Hodemaker and all those guys; they were just great, like a good mechanic. They can tell by the way your car sounds what's wrong with it.

"I'll tell you about another guy, Tiny Naylor. He wasn't in this area too much until later years, but was very successful in the Bay Area. All of these people were super in the food preparation department. They were the Mike Roys (famous chef in Los Angeles) of the restaurant industry. They had an instinct, a touch that has a certain effect on food. It's a kooky thing, but in the restaurant business I would say you've got

Henry's *Famous* Rite Spot

Sternberger's *famous* RITE SPOT SERVING FINE FOOD SINCE 1919

526 N. BRAND BLVD.
GLENDALE, CALIF.
and
6138 NORTH FIGUEROA STREET
HIGHLAND PARK, LOS ANGELES

EATON'S Santa Anita
Located at
RANCHO SANTA ANITA
ARCADIA · CALIFORNIA

Visit Eaton's Santa Anita Resort Hotel and relax in its Early California Atmosphere of hospitality and friendliness.

Car Hops & Curb Service – Jim Heimann

it or you don't, and they paid attention to details. However, even some of the successful ones eventually failed, and I think it was their inability to adjust to the sociological changes going on. Most of them couldn't see the sociological change coming; we did, and we stayed ahead of them. Bob's Big Boy was the first company that had a profit-sharing plan. Twenty percent of the net went to the employees. Everybody shared equally, including myself."

Other men came later, including Delmar Johnson, founder of Sizzler Restaurants. Johnson, a one-time ice cream salesman, knew of the success of Tad's Steak House operating in New York City, Chicago and San Francisco. They offered a steak, baked potato and salad for $1.09. He liked the concept and opened his Sizzler in Culver City in 1957. He sold franchises and eventually sold company-owned and franchisor privileges to Jim Collins and two others in 1967. Collins, the Kentucky Fried Chicken biggie, said in September 1992 that the Sizzler chain now consists of more than 700 company-owned and franchise operations valued in excess of $400 million. Recently Sizzler had serious problems, and many of the weaker units were closed.

Denny's, originally a La Mirada, California operation and now based in Spartanburg, South Carolina, is still going strong despite discrimination allegations. In 1991, Shoney's, a former Big Boy franchise, lost a similar discrimination action resulting in damages exceeding 105 million. It cost Ray Danner 60 million dollars. He could afford it as he was worth, at the time, five times as much. Danner has taken a hit recently due to stock value reverses. In 1985, Shoney's withdrew as a Marriott "Big Boy" franchise at a cost to Shoney's of 11 million.

Back to Harold Butler, founder of Denny's. At age 16, he turned a boat into a business by taking tourists for rides. Later he transformed a stack of lumber into a lumberyard. Then when he added hamburgers to his doughnut shop menu it took off, and he became one of Wall Street's favorite food operators in the mid-60's.

Carl Karcher was another original, starting in 1941 with a single hot dog cart in downtown Los Angeles. The popular Carl's Jr. has grown to 663 outlets with 14,000 employees. Unlike Bob Wian in 1967, Karcher unsuccessfully chose to battle it out with a less than cooperative board of directors in 1993.

John Dahl's Uncle John's Pancake House and Sambo's (original 1957 unit still open) created in Santa Barbara have ceased to exist and another Santa Barbara creation Carrow's has been less than effective according to recent financial reports. Oddly, another Santa Barbara area entrepeneur Paul "Kinko's" Orfalea had a similar beginning as Bob Wian. Both passionate consumer first advocates. I've never met Paul (a block away neighbor many years in Montecito, Ca.) who was, until recently, Chairman of the fabulously successful copy company. Paul is now a minor player for his creation as the new management has moved the corporate offices to Dallas, Texas and is concentrating on bottom line as their God rather than the customer as king. Like Bob's Big Boy, you take the heart out of a sole proprietorship and the possibility exists that you break the heart of the company. Some call it progress but really folks, it's greed and eventually evolves into contempt for the general public...the customer. Hopefully what happened to Big Boy will not happen to Kinko's and others who forget "what 'got 'em there."

International House of Pancakes (IHOP), a big success in their early years, changed with the times and is still prosperous with an expanded menu.

Institutions Magazine said of McDonald's Ray Kroc, "...the man who put the hamburger on a big business basis had a show biz background. Kroc began his career as a Red Cross ambulance driver with Walt Disney, put Amos and Andy on the radio, and played the piano in Florida..." We know, of course, that Kroc, who sold milk shake mixers to the McDonald brothers in San Bernardino, California, became the exclusive national franchise agent in 1956, expanded on their concept, and turned McDonald's into what it is today, with net income of over $253 million for the 1st quarter of 2002.

In the 30's and 40's, all the drug stores had soda fountains, and one of the best was the Owl Drug Store, or Rexall chain, which served a wide range of sandwiches, on white bread in those days, and great ice cream treats from bright and shiny fountain equipment. The customers sat on heavily upholstered stools that swiveled. That was really neat way to treat yourself or your favorite gal.

Now it seems the 35-year run of the fast food industry's quick service and standardized fare may be losing some steam. Most of the giants are experimenting with sit-down dining and service—Burger King, Taco Bell, Jack-In-The-Box, for example. Give them a few more years, and they will all be trying to emulate the excellence that Bob Wian attained and people like the Marriott Corporation did not know how to perpetuate. "Hamburger Heaven" The Illustrated History of the Hamburger by Jeffery Tennyson is a must read.

Those were the days, my friends!

Car Hops & Curb Service – Jim Heimann

41

TOASTED SESAME SEED BUN
(TOP)

PROPERLY AGED RED RELISH

SEA SALT

1/8 LB. FRESH
CHUCK P

PURE MAYONN

TOASTED SES
(MIDDLE)

1/8 LB. FRES
CHUCK

SLICE OF MILD
AMERICAN CHEE

SHREDDED LETTUCE

PURE MAYONNAISE

TOASTED SESAME SEED BUN
(BOTTOM)

The Original Double-DeckHamburger

BIG BOY, THE ORIGINAL DOUBLE-DECK HAMBURGER

The Original Recipe

There are 14 steps to make a Big Boy Hamburger, which consists of:

Two patties of freshly ground chuck
A sesame seed bun sliced twice
A slice of American cheddar (mild)
Shredded lettuce
Pure mayonnaise
Red relish properly aged
Sea salt
Tissue wrap
Glassine bag to cover most of the Big Boy

First, the sliced bun is placed on a grill used only for toasting Big Boy buns. Next, the patties are placed on the grill. As the meat cooks, the sliced bun is toasted, and as the meat patties and middle bun are turned over, the bottom bun is removed and spread with mayonnaise. The mayonnaise applied should elicit a slight scraping sound, as an improperly toasted bun is just soft bread harboring pockets of mayonnaise, creating a soggy, mushy sandwich. The bottom bun is then covered with shredded lettuce on which is placed a slice of mild cheddar and a meat pattie.

By then the center bun is toasted on both sides, one of which is spread with mayonnaise, followed by another meat patty sprinkled lightly with sea salt (the salt must be uniformly applied to the meat before the relish so that it will melt into the patty), with red relish (green relish blended with catsup and of course additional secret ingredients) generously centered on the meat. Finally, the top bun, now well toasted, is placed on the top of the relish. To keep the heat and the mayonnaise, relish, and meat drippings tidy, the Big Boy is then half-wrapped in tissue and placed in a four color, glassine Big Boy bag.

The bun has sesame seeds on the top, bottom and sides, and is perfectly sliced to ensure proper toasting and dressing application. In addition, the bun recipe includes enough sugar to enhance toasting characteristics. The bun must be warm-to-hot, which brings out the aroma of the toasted sesame seeds and guarantees a Big boy with crunch, which is what separates the Big Boy from all the imitators. You're biting into a sandwich with hot meat, mild to sweet dressings, cool lettuce, warm cheese, on a grilled sesame seed bun. Delicious!

Until the early 70's, it took three experienced cooks approximately 90 seconds to prepare six Big Boy hamburgers. Here's how it went. Cook #1, the "Bun Burner", put the 18 bun pieces (6 buns sliced twice) on a 2-foot by 3-foot grill, bottoms on the first row, centers on the second row, and lids (tops) on the top row. At the same time the buns were started, Cook #2 placed the meat on a 2-foot by 2-foot meat griddle, two patties per bun. During the busiest hours daily from 11:30 - 2:00, nights from 5:00 - 9:30, till 1:00 a.m. on Friday, and nearly all day Saturday and Sunday, the meat and bun grills were filled. These two grills were never used for any other purpose. The Big Boy side of the kitchen was exclusively hamburger territory.

As the first row of patties cooked, Cook #1 removed the six bun bottoms and placed them to the left of Cook #3. At the same time the meat patties were turned over by Cook #2, who fed Cook #3 bottom buns well-toasted with mayonnaise spread uniformly over all. Cook #1 then placed the center bun left to Cook #3, who spread the mayo on as Cook #2 added the lettuce and cheese to the bottoms. Cook #2 then placed six more patties on the center buns, sprinkling sea salt in a single uniform pass six inches overhead, as Cook #3 generously spooned the relish on the center of the meat. Cook #1 placed the fully-toasted top to the right of Cook #2, and Cook #3 placed the tops on the six Big Boys, and the sandwich was compete.

As the tops were placed on the relish, Cook #2 half-wrapped the Big Boy, tucking the excess tissue underneath so that no paper protruded in a sloppy manner. The tissue wrap held everything together. Because the cheese was square, one of the corners was positioned out in the exact center of the tissue wrap. As Cook #2 finished the tissue wrap, Cook #3 read the order, which was on a wheel at eye level, and put the Big Boy in a printed glassine bag to stay warm under the heat lamps. The heat lamps were used primarily to keep the counter surface hot; the Big Boys were under the lamps no longer than a few seconds. More often, all six Big Boys would be placed on the counter at the same time. As this was done, the window man called out the drink request to the fountain boy. A similar procedure applied to the other side of the kitchen preparing all of the other items offered on the menu.

Many times I have seen Big Boy cooks work their eight hours with not more than 30 minutes away from the grill. In situations where a cook was ill, late, or dismissed, the cooks on duty would work straight through, taking no breaks during the entire shift. They were the very best and they knew it. They took pride in it; they were a team.

If you worked at Bob's, you were special. And you got very good at what you did. A bun burner might do nothing else for months before being given the opportunity to do something else in the kitchen. In 1966, my son, Guy, for years a coach for the Kansas City Royals and now with the Atlanta Braves, asked me to get him a summer job before his first semester at UCLA. I assumed he would learn how to make Big Boy hamburgers. They gave him a job all right, but not behind a grill. For ten weeks straight, he plucked the green leaves from strawberries for the famous strawberry pies at Bob's. He had red fingers until Christmas.

Great Big Boy builders were Bob Eaken, later a franchise owner in Mountain View, south of San Francisco; Len Dunagan, Glen 'Buzzy' Martin , Larry Tarizzo and Dick Ingham, a vice president, Nip Hoffman, Kent Phelps, Harry Bowers, Pat Reichstein, Glenn Martin, Roger Clark, Norm Heater, Ron Chrostowski, Dick Mayes, and many more. The best Big Boy production I ever saw was at the Space Fair at Point Mugu, a Navy base in Oxnard, California, where we used the Mobile Big Boy Bob and I designed. The three cooks did nothing but prepare Big Boys, making 340 per hour for 15 hours, 5,100 Big Boys in all. Nobody was prouder of the success than Bob Wian. He knew a Big Boy kitchen on wheels would work. He wouldn't let me get behind a grill at the restaurants, but he sure knew a good P.R. vehicle when he saw one.

Now, 5,100 times 14 = 71,400 separate steps to make 5,100 Big Boy hamburgers, a lot of work, a lot of happy customers. All this production from one 2-foot by 2-foot meat grill, one 2-foot by 3-foot bun grill, with three great Big Boy builders in an 8-foot by 16-foot mobile kitchen.

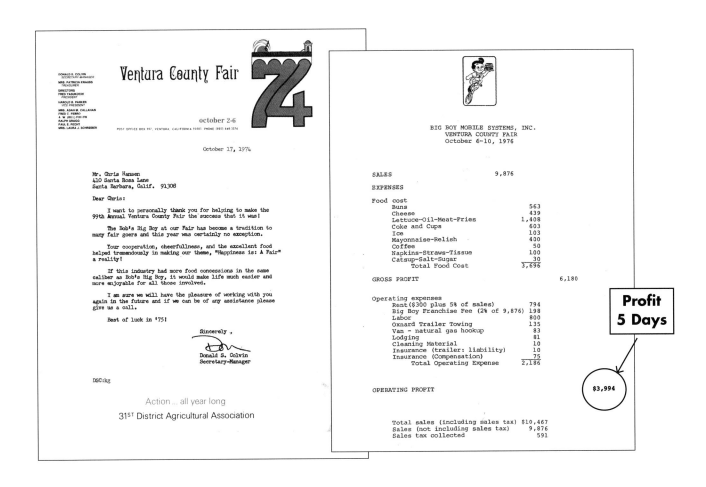

FAME, FORTUNE AND GIVING

[BOB] "Let's start back—like a long time ago. Many people inspired me to do better. I think of my Scout Master, Harvey Chessman, who, you know, while a lot of kids were whittling on a piece of wood, and I was listening to what he said, because he was older and more knowledgeable, and I thought what he said made sense. And before you can be a good talker, you've got to be a pretty good listener. You have to pick up all the things people are going to say that you feel are going to contribute, not only to your way of life, but to everybody's way of life. Harvey Chessman was one. My dad was a great inspiration. But I really think that the thing that had the most influence on my success was my association with guys in the De Molay, the 20-30 Club, and the request to lead. You don't lead by desire, you lead by request. Right? You lead because you're balloted in to lead, and then you try to embody the confidence of those that supported you to lead. And these environments—leadership, I guess, came about through the 20-30 Club and De Molay and all the organizations I was involved in. I guess it's a quest of knowledge. You've got to know what you're talking about. Right? You've got to believe in what you're trying to sell; you've got to fulfill the promises that you made; it's just a fundamental belief in what you're doing and what others can do that pulls the whole program together. Maybe I'm beating around the bush, but actually, in the restaurant business, it's not a food product. People are the product."

"Well, I don't care what side of the counter I'm seated on, there's got to be an awareness of their need to build a business. People are the product in a restaurant business, because in our business, food has got to be bought, it's got to be prepared, it's got to be served satisfactorily. You'll see the guy on the other side of the counter reflect the feeling that you put into the food you're trying to serve. It's a whole, rounded prospect. It can't be just a job; it's a life. It's not a biz; it's a life, it's really a life. And you have to have an acute awareness of the customer's needs, but not a fear."

INTERNATIONAL FOODSERVICE

CITY OF HOPE

GOLDEN PLATE AWARD

PLAQUES, TROPHIES AND MEDALS

Bob Wian, in his field, was the recipient of more commendations at an early age than anyone in the country. Of all of the awards Bob received, none were orchestrated by public relations people. Bob never tooted his own horn and was, in fact, uncomfortable with media attention. He always made sure people knew it was the employees', not the company's, contribution to the Community Chest (United Way), Salvation Army, etc. My job as a staff member was not to make Bob look good. His employees and customers took care of that. The employees stayed, and the customers kept coming back.

According to the official history of Glendale, California:

"Robert C. "Bob" Wian was best known in his home community, the City of Glendale, California, for his colorful personality which, together with hard work and a generous fund of brilliant ideas, not only gained him outstanding success, but high honors for civic mindedness."

"As a candidate for the City Council in 1948, he was elected with the largest vote ever accorded anyone seeking that office. His dedication and popularity resulted in his being chosen Mayor and, at the age of 34, was at that time one of the youngest mayors in California history."

"Permanently recorded on the city council minutes is a resolution paying tribute to him for a high sense of public responsibility, conscientious diligence and unfailing fidelity; for service consistently marked by a deep devotion to his duties and the welfare of the city and its people and adding that his industrious efforts in the conduct of public affairs have been of immeasurable value of good government in the community."

"Bob Wian's independent spirit and the initiative that had helped make him a success in business occasionally touched off fireworks in city council meetings. He assailed the time-honored closed-door sessions of the Council, declaring, 'this Council has nothing to hide and the people have a right to know what is going on. Government should be kept on the local level. The distance between government and the people is far too great."

"In 1948, Bob Wian received the rare honor of being selected by the Junior Chamber of Commerce as the Outstanding Young Man of the Year and was awarded a National Tribute for distinguished service as a civic leader; for substantial grants to his church, for scholarships given students at Glendale High School, and for welfare aid given boys with hardship problems."

A FEW NICE WORDS FROM A FEW, VERY SUCCESSFUL, GOOD FRIENDS

. . . Bob was an extraordinary person and he and I had an unusual bond from the very first day we met, in the early 1950's. I idolized him to be quite honest. He changed and influenced my life; he motivated me so strongly and gave me inspiration and confidence and taught me respect for my fellow man. To me, Bob was a symbol of what America is all about and I know many of his friends and employees felt the same way. He was indeed a special and unique individual.

Bob's business acumen was extraordinary. He was successful, honest, considerate, intelligent and a man of great compassion. He was a perfectionist who devised and practiced a unique style within the restaurant industry that had never been seen before and will probably never be repeated. "Good food, good service in impeccable surroundings" was always his motto. To this day I try to adhere to this motto in my business operations. . . . John L.N.Bitove, C.M. . . . Toronto, Ontario

. . .You've made many people happy, and many people wealthy. Of equal importance, however, you contributed to the American economy by providing so many jobs - not only in the food business, but in construction, manufacturing, marketing, finance, etc. You were a pioneer and an innovator, and a large part of the food industry today owes its success to your innovations over the past fifty years.

For what limited success has befallen me over the past 30 plus years, I owe you a debt of gratitude . . . John Mino . . . Pepper Pike, Ohio.

. . .You were indeed one of the visionaries of the modern restaurant industry and your thinking has resulted in the creation of millions of jobs and a huge industry. I marvel at how enduring and sound your concepts were and I assure you that we hold them in high regard as we confront the daily changes in our industry. . . .Stephen H Marcus . . .Milwaukee, Wisconsin

. . .Bob would go to a party and seek out the least important person at the gathering and would make that person feel like the most important one. I have seen Bob ignore Presidents of major corporations and spend much of his time talking to minor subordinates.

Bob perhaps had more foresight than any other executive I have ever seen in the restaurant field. He was one of the first ones to observe a five day work week; one of the first to pay time and a half over 40 hours; and one of the first to have a company sponsored profit sharing program. Bob had often told me you had to take care of your people that take care of you. He showed a great deal of compassion and responsibility for those who worked for him.

Bob inspired a great deal of confidence in his leadership, and his physical appearance and personality were appealing to everyone. Bob had the organization and manpower skills to be the number one restaurant operator in America. . . . Alex Azar . . .Fort Wayne, Indiana

Dear Bob,

Just a note to congratulate you on being named MUFSO's 1987 Pioneer of The Year. It's and honor richly deserved and long overdue.

You're one of the people, Bob, who make me proud to be in this industry. You've made some real contributions to our industry and to the communities that were fortunate enough to have a Big Boy located there.

This letter then is really an early thank you for all you have done for so many.

Margaret and I plan to be with you on September 29, but I didn't want to wait til then to congratulate you and give you our double-decker best wishes.

Sincerely,

Carl Karcher (Carl's Jr.)

Bob Wian, founder of Big Boy chain, chosen MUFSO Pioneer of the Year

Bob Wian in a 1979 photo.

NEW YORK — Bob Wian, the California entrepreneur who parlayed a small hamburger stand opened 51 years ago into a chain that became the Big Boy empire, has been named *Nation's Restaurant News'* 1987 Multi-Unit Food-Service Operators Pioneer of the Year.

Wian will be honored at *NRN*'s 28th annual MUFSO conference, which will be held from Sept. 27 to Sept. 30 at the Century Plaza Hotel in Los Angeles. He will receive special plaudits at the welcoming cocktail reception Sunday evening, Sept. 27, and at the annual awards banquet Tuesday evening.

MUFSO '87

Wian, who is retired and resides in Newport Beach, Calif., pioneered drive-ins and then coffee shops that grew into the Big Boy empire. He was one of the first to successfully mass-market a double-decker hamburger.

He joins *NRN*'s list of entrepreneurial pioneer honorees, including Kentucky Fried Chicken's late Col. Harlan Sanders; McDonald's late Ray Kroc; Marriott's late J. Willard Marriott Sr.; Alex Schoenbaum, a co-founder with Ray Danner of Shoney's Big Boys; Burger King's Jim McLamore; and Pizza Hut's Frank Carney.

HALL OF FAME AWARD

Bob Wian was elected a director of the National Restaurant Association, and soon afterward chosen to the elite membership selected for the American Restaurant Magazine's Hall of Fame; a distinction reserved for a select few restaurant operators excelling in purity of product and outstanding service! His La Crescenta restaurant, the number three in his fast-growing chain, was selected for the National Merit Award for meritorious achievement in food service installation design by Institutions Magazine of Chicago.

The Institutional Food Manufacturer's Association presented Bob Wian The Golden Plate Award. Bob was the third recipient of this honor awarded each year at the National Restaurant convention in Chicago.

Bob Wian was rarely critical of his associates. He did, however, feel that Big Boy franchisee Alex Schoenbaum should not have accepted the Multi-Unit Food Service Operators (MUFSO) Pioneer of the Year Award before he, Bob, was honored. Alex was not in the same league as previous winners Colonel Harland Sanders, Ray Kroc of McDonald's, and J. Willard Marriott. Bob was finally chosen for the award in 1987.

Wian Enterprises joined hands with all its employees in an unusual Community Chest contribution plan. Employees donated one full day's pay, and the company matched the employees' donation.

Among the most prized possessions hanging in the Wian home is the 'Humanitarian of the Year Award' presented by the City of Hope.

Pension Trust Fund - Profit Sharing Plan

Public recognition of Bob's accomplishments was secondary to his innovative and mutually beneficial employee relations concepts. For example,

> [BOB] "It's a life, it's a life. And it's just like your kids. You reward them for doing something good, and you scold them discreetly for doing something bad, and you try to raise a family like a family should be raised, and you run a business like a family should be run. It's the same thing. How can you—it's . . . it's . . . I can't explain it. I don't imagine that the same thing would be conceivable today, where you could sit down with a guy and say, 'I've got an idea. I think between the two of us we could do it. And if we do it, why we're going to share on the basis which is proportionate to our interests and our contribution to the thing.' And the whole thing is a sales pitch. But you've got to back up the item you're selling. Every employee we hired had a warranty; if they didn't abuse the equipment, the warranty was built in. And I guess at Bob's, there were few people who complained about the way they were treated, or about the rewards they received for the efforts they put forth. So it's a relative, fair, doing-to-others type of thing . . . and if it wasn't that way, how could you sleep at night?""

At Bob's you didn't get a gold watch when you left the company. You got a golden opportunity, whether it be the employee franchise program or the rewards provided by the Pension Trust Fund created by the profit sharing plan, and it wasn't a share-and-share-alike plan where the employer gave dollar for dollar or stock options. Bob put all the money in the fund, and the employees contributed nothing but loyalty, good performance, and faith in the future of Bob's Big Boy. Many long-time employees retired from the company with benefits exceeding hundreds of thousands. One, a waitress, left with over six hundred thousand. John Colin, a dishwasher his entire career with Bob's, left with $175,975.01. Enron, Global Crossing, and yesterdays Lincoln Savings- Keating fiasco, couldn't use a Bob's Employee Profit Sharing Plan . . . it would be just too simple in this day and age of accounting, legal, and corporate B.S. Even the 401K's might need a little WD 40 to get rid of the rust and corrosion.

Bob could be tick tight when it came to money, his money; but when it came to sharing his company's good fortune, the opposite was true.

> [BOB] "The profit-sharing was a well thought out, well-rounded program, but the first thing the Marriott's did was to change the profit-sharing picture so that down the road the program was not going to move along as originally planned."

the Enterprise

ENERGETIC
PROGRESSIVE
INVENTIVE

PUBLISHED MONTHLY BY AND FOR Bob's MORE THAN 1200 EMPLOYEES

PROFIT SHARING OVER A MILLION

PROFIT SHARING HOLDS ANNUAL MEETING

January 27, 1986

$708,310.74

Mr. Elmo L. Geoghegan
1009 E. Mountain
Glendale, Ca. 91207

Dear Elmo:

Your interest in the Employee's Profit Sharing Plan as of December 31, 1984 was $615,463.58. On the date of your retirement December 27, 1985, the net worth of the Plan had increased 13.88% due primarily to the changes in the value of our listed and traded stocks. This means that on your retirement date your account showed $700,889.92.

You are 100% vested, therefore we are enclosing Check #3826 in the amount of $708,310.74 which represents your vested interest and also includes your 1985 Company Contribution in the amount of $7,420.82.

Please let us remind you that these funds are taxable for income tax purposes under the Federal and State Law in the following manner. The portion of the distribution attributable to the number of months of your participation prior to 1974 is treated as capital gain. The portion of the distribution attributable to the number of months of your participation after 1973 is treated as ordinary income.

To comply with the above, distribution is as follows:

$708,310.74 X months before 1974 = 324 = $490,368.97
total months active = 468 = Capital Gain

$708,310.74 X months after 1973 = 144 = $217,941.77
total months active = 468 = Ordinary Income

The preceding computations are in accordance with our understanding of the current provisions of the law. Your Federal and State Information Returns will be forwarded to you as soon as they are available.

Sincerely,

EMPLOYEES' PROFIT SHARING PLAN
OF BOB'S BIG BOY

Dorothy Long
Dorothy Long
Treasurer

DL/ly
By Certified Mail

*Elmo started out
at Bob's as
a kitchen helper!
-C.H.*

The Employees' Profit Sharing Plan of Robert C. Wian Enterprises, Inc., held its annual meeting on March 4 in the Auditorium of the General Office Building.

Leonard A. Dunagan, Chairman of the Board of Trustees of the "Plan" presided over the meeting — as usual a large percentage of the members were present to hear the annual report.

The minutes of the previous meeting were read by Secretary Elmo Geoghegan. The financial report was given by the Treasurer, Ruth McAdoo.

Chairman Dunagan extended "Greetings" to all the members from Bob Wian, who was on vacation in Mexico. Donn Boyle, Board Member from Phoenix, also greeted the members on behalf of all of those in Phoenix.

The four-year terms of Board Members, Leonard Dunagan, Ruth McAdoo, and Robert Eakin had expired; attorney Fred Chase, member of the Board of Trustees, presided over the election of new members to the Board. All three members were re-elected to another four-year term.

The "Profit Sharing Plan" was initiated by Bob Wian many years ago because he felt that management should be concerned with the retirement plans of its employees. It is the only "Plan" of its kind in the restaurant industry.

All employees with five years of seniority with the Company be-

Roger Wilson/Glendale **News-Press**

Waitress Betty Santoro gives Bob's Big Boy a hug on her last day on the job at the restaurant.

'Temporary' job ends 34 years later

BOB'S BIG BOY PROFIT SHARING PLAN
PATICIPANTS' ACCOUNTS
12/31/91

PARTICIPANT	BALANCE 12/31/90	1991 PAYOFF	SHARE OF CONTRIB- UTION
BOCK, CORA(MABLEY)	92,595.16		2,992.42
DUENAS, ARISTEO	244,772.07		1,483.36
FITZPATRICK, STUART	244,772.07		8,606.51
HALLOCK, CHARLES	244,772.07		8,606.51
HEATER, HELEN	194,195.04	200,804.86	7,761.34
HEATER, JOHN	280,919.11		8,606.51
HOGAN, CHARLES	214,027.59		8,606.51
LONG, DOROTHY	219,966.99		0.00
LORIMOR, MARIE	172,686.91		3,731.20
MAYES, RICHARD	233,766.52		8,606.51
MONTGOMERY, PATRICIA	99,594.11		4,363.82
NOVODOCZKY, RONALD	280,919.11		8,606.51
SANCHEZ, RICHARD	203,573.00		8,606.51
SANCHEZ, DAVID	203,573.00		8,606.51
SANTORO, BEATRICE	**246,113.32**	**255,172.01**	**2,758.08**
TUESBURG, BONNIE	104,491.67		3,603.12
VINCENT, SHIRLEY	133,977.29		3,130.96
WARREN, CHAROLET	224,028.91		8,606.51
WHALEN, ROBERT	203,572.75		8,606.51
	3,842,316.69	455,976.87	115,889.40

John W. Colin
6817 Woodley Avenue
Van Nuys, Ca. 91406

Dear John:

Your interest in the Employee's Profit Sharing Plan as of December 31, 1984 was $157,782.67. On the date of your termination, November 10, 1985, the net worth of the Plan had increased due primarily to the changes in the value of our listed and traded stocks. This means that on your termination date your account showed $175,975.01.

You are 100% vested, therefore we are enclosing Check #3822 in the amount of $175,975.01 which represents your vested interest.

Please let us remind you that these funds are taxable for income tax purposes under the Federal and State Law in the following manner. The portion of the distribution attributable to the number of months of your participation prior to 1974 is treated as capital gain. The portion of the distribution attributable to the number of months of your participation after 1973 is treated as ordinary income.

To comply with the above, distribution is as follows:

$$\$175,975.01 \times \frac{\text{months before 1974}}{\text{total months active}} = \frac{156}{299} = \$91,813.05 \quad \text{Capital Gain}$$

$$\$175,975.01 \times \frac{\text{months after 1973}}{\text{total months active}} = \frac{143}{299} = \$84,161.96 \quad \text{Ordinary Income}$$

The preceeding computations are in accordance with our understanding of the current provision of the law. Your Federal and State Information Returns are enclosed.

In addition to this lump sum distribution, if it is determined that you have completed 1000 hours, you may be entitled to receive your share of this year's company contribution, which will be distributed next year.

Sincerely,

EMPLOYEE'S PROFIT SHARING PLAN
OF BOB'S BIG BOY

Richard G. Ingham
Richard G. Ingham
Secretary

RGI/ly
Enclosures by Certified Mail

*That's $175,975.01 -
John spent his entire career
at Bob's as a diswasher!!*
-C.H.

Central & Thomas, Phoenix, Ariz.

THE EMPLOYEE
FRANCHISE PLAN

[BOB] "Gave the guy who starts today a chance to be in business for himself a few years down the road as a brighter horizon to look forward to, and it kept the momentum going through the ranks, kept enthusiasm going through the people who were eager to learn. Maybe they could use the knowledge in their own business someday. I think it was the most absolutely fantastic thing. There was so much territory in the West that we were incapable of developing and administering it properly. A franchise program was one way of expanding the opportunities in the West."

From the Bob's Big Boy house organ, The Enterprise:

In the interest of rewarding key employees and as a motivating factor in developing management personnel, the company feels that it is essential to have a well-defined, consistent management-franchising program.

Asa Finnel, Harry Andrews, Alex Goodman, Ray Gray
The Phoenix Fearsome Foursome and Associates

Goodfellows Club

The Goodfellows Club was so called because the produce supplier was named Goodfellow. As a gesture of good will and personnel relations he and Bob set up a special night, once a month, for the male employees to gather for cards, food, fellowship. They had Vegas-type games, and the winners would receive prizes donated by suppliers. The first meetings were held in the Goodfellow home, and later in the main office waitress training area. It would start right after the day shift was off duty and continue right through the night as the night shift would come in about 1 A.M. and stay until 5 or 6 A.M. The events provided 24 hours of entertainment and fellowship, which gave the employees an opportunity to learn more about their co-workers from the other restaurants.

Turkey Trot

The Turkey Trot was a Thanksgiving Day party and dance for all employees.

Bidder Halves

The Bidder Halves was a Bridge club for wives of staff members, including luncheon at a well-known restaurant with prizes, luncheon and bridge instructions, etc.

Bob's Employees Association

Bob's Employees Association was unique in that it was a National Labor Relations Board-approved union for a regional restaurant operation. It qualified because Robert C. Wian Enterprises wholly owned the L. A. Dunagan Company, a shrimp brokerage selling surplus shrimp interstate.

Junior Executives Club

The Junior Executives Club was a program designed to acquaint assistant store managers with the responsibilities of executive positions. All participated although it was not mandatory.

DOUBLE EAGLE

Bob's menu was famous for entrees other than the Big Boy, and the shrimp dinner was the second most popular. Shrimp were caught by a fleet of 15 boats under contract to Bob in the Gulf of California, and the best part of the catch was kept for Bob's Restaurants. The schooner Double Eagle, the ship used in "The Wackiest Ship in the Army" TV series, was originally purchased to help guarantee a supply of shrimp to the restaurants, but it eventually became a favorite employee benefit.

There were years when the catch was so plentiful that the shrimp operation helped the bottom line of the restaurants. The excess was brokered around the world at considerable profit. There were also some bad times, however, when the shrimp gathering expense became a major factor in the decision to sell or merge Big Boy with others. In 1965 and 1966, after advances of over a million dollars to pay for crew, fuel, nets, boat rehab, etc., with no shrimp being caught, the pressure was put on Bob by certain members of his corporate Board to give up the reins or at least bring about a new business philosophy of running Big Boy in Southern California and expanding to other areas.

The 90-foot gaff schooner was scouting for shrimp beds in the Gulf when the Mexican Government got wind of the practice and stopped further use of a United States registry boat for shrimp bed location. Bob subsequently used the boat in an employee relations R&R program. At least once a year, all the store managers were invited to spend a couple of days at sea. The managers would arrive in Newport Beach or Balboa Island at midnight, board a fishing boat for a trip to Catalina Island, twenty-five miles off the California coast. Once there, they were transferred to the Double Eagle for breakfast, a fishing tournament, and fish fry. On the way back to the mainland, guests were served 16-ounce steaks, baked potato, sour cream and chives, salad—the works..

When the guests were let off on the mainland, the boat turned around and went back to Catalina. This would go on for ten days. Bob cooked every meal, over 500 of them, by

Xmas, Bob —
a hell of a
but hard to catch!
Frankie Alluoto

himself, and most times didn't leave the galley except for pictures with the guys up on deck during the trophy awards. But while he was on duty in the galley, he was accessible to anyone to discuss any subject that was on the minds of the men who made things like the Double Eagle possible. On other occasions, the Double Eagle was a business boat entertaining suppliers, supermarket executives, staff members, wives and charitable organizations. Bob had not forgotten what he had learned from his Scoutmaster about contributing to other people's lives.

Bob had more than shrimp in mind when he bought the boat, and in 1966 he and Skipper Bob Sloan followed the Trans Pac race to Hawaii, taking along his son, Chappie, sons of other friends, along with Dr. George Towne, a good friend of Bob's for 40 years. The crossing had some high drama when a guest, DeForest "Pappy" Lawrence, developed a very serious illness. Dr. Towne did everything he could to help, but eventually had to call the Coast Guard cutter Dexter for more exotic medical supplies. When he learned the cutter was 35 hours away; all hope was lost for the dying shipmate. Assistance came in the form of a Navy bomber, which located the Double Eagle and made a drop of a 55-gallon drum of medical supplies. The Coast Guard had notified Honolulu to assist the Double Eagle. Much later Dr. Towne learned that Pappy Lawrence, his patient, was the son-in-law of the former Secretary of the Navy and one-time Ambassador to China.

John Mino, long-time franchisee in Cleveland, taught us how to lose graciously on the Double Eagle playing a card game called In Between. John said, "Three cards are dealt to each player. The object of this game is to receive a card in between the lowest and the highest card in your hand. An ace, a deuce, and three is the winning hand. After the initial three cards are dealt, you can stand pat, or you can discard one or two cards in an attempt to improve your hand, raising your bet if your new cards appear to be winners. I remember one night on the Double Eagle when I beat Dave Frisch out of a $400 pot. Dave never played the game again."

Opposite page: (center) Bob Wian; (bottom right) Bob & Pappy Wian with Joe Scalzo and friends; (bottom left) famed Stanford and San Francisco 49ers Quarterback Frankie Albert writes: "Merry Xmas, Bob – You're a hell of a man but hard to catch!"; Wian portrait photographer - Roy Raskin. Above: June & Bob; (Right) Ingrid & Bobby.

LEN "BOSS" DUNAGAN AND OTHERS

Many people were associated with Bob over the years. He knew their value and appreciated their relationships. This chapter identifies some of them, relying primarily on Bob's own words.

[BOB] "Every restaurant has two doors, the back and the front. You've got to have somebody that watches the back and somebody to take care of the people who come in the front. It's a tricky thing, because it's so complicated sometimes. There are so many facets to it, and you have to be almost self-educated in all of them. Even at those restaurant forums they have at the National Restaurant Association and places like that, most of the people on the platform really don't know what they're talking about, because the ones who are successful are too damned busy and probably a little too selfish to share all their secrets."

The late Len Dunagan was Bob Wian's manager at Sternberger's in 1935. Bob opened his own place in 1936 and in 1937 convinced Len to come over to Big Boy to help run things. Bob said of Len,

[BOB] "Len Dunagan was the greatest employer that I had, the greatest associate I ever had. He was so positive, sincere; he had integrity beyond question, and he always did his best."

"Now any person has limitations, but doing your best is all you can ask of one. Right? But Dunagan was one guy that set the pace for the company that we built. Leonard Dunagan was the greatest and so busy with what he was doing that he didn't have time to give pleasant overtures to people. But he was a craftsman. He got the job done like a guy that's finishing furniture: you don't dare talk to him when he's putting on the finishing touch. It had to go out right, and fast. His relationships with the customer and the people who worked for him were none too good, but he set the standards for the craft. Dunagan was the real inspiration. One time he quit in the middle of World War II when the only cooks we had were the guys with a bottle of wine in the back seat of their car. In the meantime, I was trying to fill in where the vacancies were, and doing my job at the 20-30 Club. The guys from 17 to 27 years old were all gone, I was 26 and a 4-F, and nobody was left behind to keep the thing going, so I used to travel all over Southern California looking for the right people to keep the thing alive. So, one night I got back about 1:00 o'clock in the morning. Dunagan had just closed the joint and said, "I gotta talk to you." I said, "Okay, come up to the office." It was obvious Len had a lot on his mind, but he was too nervous to make a big speech. He just said, "I quit." He was making $60 a week at the time. I said, "Okay, boss." I always called him boss. "You're quitting?" "Yes," he said, "I'm through—tired, bushed, prices are just ridiculous." I said, "Well, I've been trying to build a business,

Front Row — Left to Right: Caroline Morrison, Lorraine Gauthier, Audrey Vercilli, Eleanor Pursley, Jan Stevenson, Berjie Jouroyan, Doris Hoveland, Virginia Whitley, Lois Jackson, Lena Bonifield.
Back Row — Left to Right: Cunard Nelson, Davis Wood, Elmo Geoghegan, Leonard Dunagan, Robert C. Wian, Thomas Holman, Ed Melton, Kenneth Dowson, Asst. Office Mgr., Paul Moore.

right? And you've been with me over two years." I wrote him a check for $30,000. I only had $40,000 in the bank. I gave him the check for $30,000 and said, "Here's your interest for the business. This is what you earned over and above what I've been able to pay you." He started to cry, tore up the check, and we never had another talk about quitting..

"This guy had done so much toward starting things, and we had earned an image that was super. Dunagan was the greatest, but there were others. A year after I opened, I got an attack of ulcers, so my dad got my mom to come to work for us when Dad told Mom, 'Bob's bleeding.' But I would say if there's one person, with everybody else's help, Dunagan was the greatest; he set the pace. He set the standards for everybody. He came to work—he was immaculate..

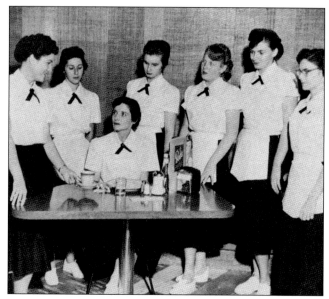

"Our years of association were most pleasant. We had many personal discussions—you know, things that affected both of us about the business; and I guess if either of us has matured any, it's because of the discussions we had. I remember the first time Len came in the office. He was manager one night, and the next day was promoted to supervision, and he came in the office to chat. We were sitting there, and a woman called up on the phone. She said, "Are you Bob Wian?", and I said, "Yup." She said, "You've got a manager on that Colorado Street place that's the meanest, most miserable person I've ever known in my life." And I said, "Just a minute, lady." I said, "Len, pick up the other phone." I said, "Yes, Ma'am, now what were you saying?" She said, "You've got a manager down there with a mustache, and he bawls out the waitresses in front of people, and I just can't stand him.""

"That's the most valuable lesson Len ever learned about cooks hassling the waitresses; there was a perfect example, right on the phone. He heard about himself. Boy, he could sure dish it out.

"My dad, a gregarious, friendly man, went into the kitchen at No.1 to visit. In the early days, waitresses called in the orders—there were no sales checks. Len Dunagan must have had 25 orders he was keeping track of in his head, and when my dad tried to engage in small talk, Len lost his concentration and didn't know who ordered what. He gave my dad holy hell. I told Len, 'You can't talk to my father that way.' Pappy and Len didn't speak for years..

"Another kitchen experience. When I worked in the kitchen with Len, I would, at times, leave the knife on its cutting edge in a vertical position. Len warned me many times to knock it off. 'You're going to cut my God-damned fingers off.' Well, it happened again, and Len was badly cut. He told my dad that if I ever came into the kitchen again he

was through. I never went back in the kitchen. I washed a few thousand dishes and all the rest, but I never again put a cook's apron on in a Big Boy Restaurant. Len said to Pappy, 'If Bob puts an apron on again in this kitchen, I'll leave.'"

It wasn't a legend that Len Dunagan would place a new cook's hand palm down on a hot grill in an effort for the new employee to lose his fear of fingertip burns. It was meant to be constructive, and in an age where there were ten people in line to get every job, he was probably doing a lot of young men a big favor.

[BOB] "He was tough. He set the standards. We just changed the way it was administered. He did it by demand and example. I did it by persuasion—a little different way, like selling. Len's selling job would be, "You dumb son of a bitch," you know. "You mean you can't learn to turn a God-damned egg?" You could hear him all over the place, but boy, he was a super man on a grill. Geez, he could have 50

63

Florence and Elmo...Teammates

orders and know just how everybody wanted them cooked. But you did-
n't dare talk to him while he was working. Boy, he was like a machine..

Len Dunagan retired in 1969, 32 years after starting with Bob. He lived with his wife
Dottie on the Kern River, site of the Olympic Games kayak competition in 1984. One the
Dunagans' neighbors in Kernville is Bob's sister Dottie.

    [BOB] Len Dunagan was responsible for a lot of real artists—
Ace Finnell, Alex Goodman, Tommy Holman, many guys who worked
with Len in the technical aspect of it. Super, super men in the kitchen. I
mentioned Tommy Holman. He had the most natural attributes toward
the employees. I would say he had a visual and intuitive sense about
people's behavior. [He could] tell whether a waitress is smiling by the
way her ears wiggle, the look of her from the back—tell whether a waitress is treating a customer right by the expression on the customer's
face. Tommy was a very fine restaurant man.

    "Florence Hansen was a contributor. Well, more than that. She was
more than a contributor was; she was, well, I don't know how to....

Nobody could do what Florence Hansen did. Nobody! Just super! And to do it time and time again, with the same enthusiasm in her position with the waitresses and hostesses. And she doesn't do it like a recording, but with feeling; and she means it. But to maintain this type of drive and sincerity—just super. You take Florence Hansen on the floor, Len Dunagan on the grill, and any one of a hundred guys in the dish tank, washing dishes by hand, and you could do so much business you couldn't believe it.

Florence was food service manager. She was in charge of training of all food service people at every franchise location, going out with the task forces whenever a new store opened. If you liked the service in a Big Boy restaurant, it was because Florence carried out Bob's wishes for customer satisfaction.

[BOB] "One of the most capable people in our company was Ruth MacAdoo [vice president and treasurer], and she could have been most anything if she wasn't a woman. I don't say that because of her sex, but because of her emotional approach to certain situations. She really was a great contributor to the whole thing.

"And another guy is Russell "Little Rusty" Hanabal. He used to go to work in the morning and peel 10 sacks of potatoes with one of those hand peelers. When he got finished, because of the starch, he was completely white. I mean, he was a Caucasian, but I mean as white as your tennis shoes. He'd sit there on the floor and go at those damned potatoes, and they had to be done. But who could sit there and peel 10 sacks of potatoes? It takes a certain guy to do it."

Tommy Holman was for many years the Oklahoma Big Boy franchisee before returning west as a consultant to major food service operators. He and Len remained very close to Bob, taking at least one trip a year to Baja, Mexico, in their four-wheel drive pickups. When I asked Len in 1993 what they did on the ten-day excursions, he said, and this was typical of Len, "Oh, just sat around the campfire and shot the breeze". Len Dunagan never asked for credit in helping to develop the young men, including Tommy, who in most cases became very successful with their own franchises, but they knew and placed great value in their relationship with "the boss."

[BOB] "A leader is someone who can get more out of people than they can get out of themselves. They had tremendous pride working at Bob's. It was truly a family. Young men found a home at Big Boy and they took pride in their endurance rather than self pity in the hard work and demanding environment".

The Phoenix Fearsome Foursome was Alex Goodman, Asa Finnell, Harry "The Bear"

Andrews, and Ray Gray. When Bob put this first employee franchise group together in 1955, he didn't miss a trick. The balance of talent was ingenious, each one very strong, but in different ways. Two supervisors; one a tiger, the other cool, calm and collected. Two store managers; one highly-skilled from a big Bob's Coffee Shop and Drive-In combination, the other, the oldest, a low-key, mature pro, with extensive coffee shop experience.

Ed Melton took his franchise on Balboa Island in the Newport Beach area. He was a veteran coffee shop and drive-in manager who was more than happy to slow down to a small but very prosperous tourist area coffee shop.

In Tucson, the mix was similar to that of the Phoenix boys. It was a little less structured because of the size of the city, but nevertheless a great combination in Milton Spencer, Dick Golson, and Bruce Bryfogle. Milt, a long-time manager at No.2 in Burbank, was the first to hear my idea to have a Big Boy Comic Book. Years later Manfred Bernhard sold the concept to all of the franchisees, and it became the most successful marketing tool on a nationwide scale that Big Boy ever had. Manfred, a great friend of Bob and all of the Big Boy family, managed to put together a package that everyone would promote and profit by.

The Fresno, California, franchise met with tragedy so traumatic that the operation never realized its potential. Its lead guy, Jack Nyemaster, a 6'4", 210-pound ex-Marine who couldn't swim, was drowned, along with his wife, Adele, in their swimming pool after work on one of Fresno's hot and humid summer nights. Adele perished trying to save her husband.

Bill Freeman and Bill Walker were the partners with Jack. Freeman, a great guy, eventually went to work as an executive for the Mark's Big Boy Franchise in the Midwest. Several people opened franchises in northern California. Harry Matthews, Clyde Smith, and Phil Schmidt went to San Jose. Bob Eaken, Bill Bellamy, and Gil Le Francois to Mountain View. Carl Thornton, Chuck Halleck, and Bob Rinehardt went to Fremont; Jim Gibson, Dal Dungan, and Don Schumacker went to Concord. Most sold out to Marriott and retired well to do and live the good life. They earned it. Many others eligible for a franchise chose to stay with the company and accumulate additional pension trust fund dollars. The Marriott merger agreement did include some of Bob's employee benefits, particularly for the last of the core group. If any one person could have made Marriott's involvement in Big Boy more successful, it was Carl Thornton, who was highly respected by everyone in the Big Boy family.

There were hundreds more who made Big Boy the best. How do you give credit where credit is due? All you can say is that if you worked and grew with Bob Wian and his philosophy of making the customer king, you acquired a principle that would pay off for the rest of your life regardless of your career objectives.

Other major contributors to Bob's success included Don Fagan, Bob Glassett, John Barringer, Larry Kunz, Roy Raskin, Stan Goodman, Ed Glassett, Mickey Erskine, Howard Rickard, and a cast of thousands.

The following is excerpted from a letter sent to me in the spring of 1993 by Florence Hansen, who was by then retired and living with her husband in Spanish Fork, Utah. (Her husband has since died, and she is now Mrs. Canaan.)

"Service with a smile"

"He [Bob Wian] was so far ahead of his time. When I started to work for him, at 24, he was already giving paid vacations to his employees. Shortly after, we got sick pay for five (5) days a year if it was needed. As I was in my fifth year, he started a profit sharing program for everyone. We put nothing into it but a good honest day's work. At the end of the year, he took a portion of his profits and gave them to the employees. It was this seed money that allowed some of his long term managers and supervisors to start their own franchises. He knew everyone by his or her first names. As he walked through the units, he would stop and say hi to each one and ask how we were doing.

"He did so much to upgrade the image of restaurant personnel. He advertised for cashiers and hostesses and talked them into becoming waitresses. He wanted young, attractive, quick-moving, pleasant front-end people.

"We were taught the customer is always 'king.' In fact, he said, 'I would rather you steal from me than to offend one of my customers'.

"If there were problems to be solved, he would listen carefully to everyone involved and then make up his mind, and it was almost impossible to get him to change it.

"He was so thoughtful and caring about his help. I remember once a franchise employee had an emergency at home. There were no flights available, so Bob rented a private plane and sent another employee along with her to make sure she got home safely, and he told her not to tell anyone about it. He was that kind of man.

"No wonder everyone that worked for him loved him. We counted one day that we had 54 years' seniority working on one shift.

"He lived by his creed: 'Good food at fair prices, clean restaurants, and prompt, courteous service,' as well as a great company to work for.

"One last thing—he was the first to give women an opportunity to prove they could handle executive positions. No wonder we all loved him.'"

His employees revered Bob Wian to the point of idolatry. However, his stubbornness was confusing to many. He would listen to other points of view, but rarely would gentle persuasion or head-knocking debate alter his thinking. Getting Bob to change his mind was like trying to teach someone to tap dance on a lawn. In many ways Bob was a very complex fellow. If you hired a psychologist to figure out Bob's personality or characteristics, it wouldn't be long before the psychologist would need a psychiatrist.

The guy was magic, always arriving on his workdays around 10 a.m. Everybody immediately felt better. He was what every employee dreamed about: the perfect boss.

Nobody was afraid, suspicious, or intimidated by Bob. He could make everything right just by his presence.

I used to stop by his home (designed by famed architect Paul Williams) in Toluca Lake on my way to the office. His family saw more of me than they wanted, but due to ignorance on my part I didn't break the habit. He would always be in his den, a beautifully wood-paneled room, 30 x 50 feet with a round mahogany card table with overstuffed swivel chairs, sofas, coffee tables, and of course a walk-in bar. He had a beautiful view of the lake and other lakeside estates. Directly across were Bobby Darin and Sandra Dee. Next door, Roy Disney, Walt's nephew and head of Shamrock. Many times, Bob's very close friend, Barney Dale, Dale's supermarkets, would be there on his way to his office looking for an excuse not to go. Barney was Jewish but around Bob, who was surrounded by every ethnicity, there were no minorities...only Americans of Jewish, Latin, African, et al descent. I never, ever, heard Bob belittle a so called minority or one less fortunate due to a disability.

Bob's wife June was responsible for the elegance and good taste. Her artistic talent also was that of an accomplished painter, portraits particularly. It was a comfortable place to be. Who wouldn't want to be there?

"The Back Yard"
9956 Toluca Lake Avenue, Toluca Lake

BOB WAS A METHODIST BUT HIS RELIGION WAS RELATIONSHIPS

Bob was never a phony in praise of associates. You might get a kick in the pants, but seldom a pat on the back; however, if someone else had complimented your work, he would pass it on in the simplest of terms. Example: "Nice." No handshake, no gratuitous B.S. He knew what you were capable of.

Bob was fanatically protective of the restaurant employees. From dishwashers to managers, supervisors to vice presidents, they were his people, the stars of the show. The others—office workers, CPA's, legal counsel (William "Bill" Gray, later to become a US District Judge)—were merely spear-carriers employed to keep the numbers and legal situations in check. Simply put, if you were in food preparation at the commissary, or in cooking and service at the restaurants, you were special to Bob.

As an employee, you never heard Bob refer to you as the help, someone who works for me. You were always introduced as an associate. You worked with Bob, not for Bob. He brought a dignity to former losers, used-to-bes, and never-wases that transcended reality; and it worked, because you never felt you were being patronized or manipulated. The only person that was ever called "Boss" in the entire organization was Len Dunagan, and that moniker was used only when Bob was talking to Len. All this may sound like a bunch of bull, but it was really that way. The people who were closely associated with Bob never met, before or after, an employer who was as unique and innovative in his treatment of his associates. Bob even gave his executive staff $200 per month for the express purpose of benefiting employees seen eating out. If an executive staff member saw an employee and family, or an employee and spouse or date, eating out anywhere, he was to pay the bill cheerfully but without fanfare.

Bob was very protective of his staff. The restaurant guys might make passes at the female employees, but if it happened in an aggressive manner it usually means sayonara, see you later, you're looking for work.

Customer and personnel relations were Bob's most important products. Every complaint, if in writing, was acknowledged with an individually typed letter of explanation, apology or thank you. If the customer suggested there had been a menu item that was inferior, or if the customer suggested a better way of doing something, that customer received a letter and coupon book for future use. On the back of every sales check were questions regarding service, food quality and courtesy. The customer was king, and Bob never forgot it. Never

ever did he try to put something over on the customer. He didn't know how to be devious, opportunistic or greedy. He had a system that worked. Why fool with it? For example, in the 60's, only four new items were added to the menu: chicken, strawberry pie, soup, and pecan pie. The pecan pie was added after years of discussion. But here is an example of Bob's philosophy on being a step ahead of the industry: Bob, while serving a generous slice of pecan pie at a very modest price, added a dollop of whipped cream to the piece of pie. Then, on the center of the topping, he put a half Maraschino cherry placed precisely so that the cut half was on the whipped cream. So the customer not only got the pie at a great price, but also got the bonus of a beautifully prepared dessert for which most restaurants would charge

Maryland 1967 - Elmo Goehegan, Chris Hansen, Marti & Bill Bemis and Bob Wian.

at least twice as much. It really wasn't a big deal; it was simply giving the customer a better bargain with the whipped cream and cherry.

Somebody, in describing Bob's pricing policy said, "You couldn't get screwed at Bob's." It was true. Every single item was fairly priced; the portions were always generous; the service was terrific; you ate in super clean surroundings; and the food was delicious. No wonder Bob's was the best. Everybody knew it, particularly the personnel who demanded the best from themselves because, from the top down, it was the only way to do it.

A quick story. It's 1955, Friday, 7 p.m., at the Toluca Lake Coffee Shop and

Drive-In. There's a line up in the coffee shop and drive-in that would last for hours.

Bob, along with supervisor Alex Goodman, who later became part of the original employee franchise in Phoenix, once walked into the kitchen area and spotted a waitress who had a tense and/or less than pleasing expression on her face. Bob said to Alex, "Is she all right?" Without missing a beat and with none of the day crew still around to fill in, Alex mentioned the situation to the manager Ed Melton, who immediately had other service personnel double up, sent the waitress home, and no one, not even the rest of the crew, knew or inquired what caused the change or why. In other words, you never brought your personal problems to work, particularly for the customer to see. The waitress returned to work the next

Minot, ND - Bob Wian, Margaret & Harley McDowell, Colonel E. P. Knox, Manfred Bernhard
Background: "June Bug" Aero Commander

evening, with no questions, no guilt trip, no problem.

In February 1968, at the Century Plaza Hotel in Los Angeles, after the merger with Marriott, all of the Marriott principals, including wives, were attending a black-tie, silver-service dance, in order to formally meet Big Boy owner/operators from across the country. It was my assignment to introduce Bob, who would welcome the Marriott's to the Big Boy Family. "Good evening, ladies and gentlemen. It is my distinct honor and privilege to introduce Robert C. 'Bob' Wian. In my view, Mr. Wian has contributed more to the food service industry than anyone. In addition, this humanitarian to all mankind continues to shine like a beacon light from (long pause as I looked around the room back to Bob, back to the room with an exasperated look, then back to Bob). Holy smokes! Bob, do I have to say these things? Give me a break; give it a rest; time out (hand signal). Don't just sit there, Wian; come up here and say hello to the folks."

Bob laughed and so did everybody else. Even on the most formal occasions, Bob appreciated a good gag, even when he took the hit. Anyone who knew Bob was well aware that the praise over the years got to be a little much and he grew to truly dislike tributes of any type, regardless of the sincerity or purpose. He knew who he was and what he had accomplished.

Bob's aversion to attention was well-illustrated at the close of a Frisch convention in Cincinnati. As was normal on these occasions, the last evening called for black tie dinner dance with toasts, tributes and a speech or two. Bob begged off, saying we had to get out quickly as the weather forecast was not good for flying the following day. Our host agreed, and we checked out of the hotel. When we got to the airport, Colonel E. P. Knox, pilot of our Aero Commander, informed us that the front had moved in earlier than expected. We had some choices: take a commercial flight, wait it out at the airport, go back to the hotel where the dinner dance was being held, or check into another hotel downtown and hide. We did the latter. We couldn't take a chance on being seen by any of the hundred or so guests at the convention, or questions would be asked as to why we did not attend the dinner. Five of us sat in that hotel suite for two days, ate all our meals in the room, and used up all our clean clothes, thinking that any minute the weather would lift and we could clear out. Finally, on the third day, Colonel Knox said we could make it, and we checked out of the hotel at 6:00 a.m. to avoid being seen. All this was because Bob did not want to make a speech, accept a tribute, or be asked to dance with ladies he barely knew. He also didn't wish to create an awkward situation with Dave Frisch and Jack Maier, who were always very hospitable. In fact, they were the only franchisee that invited Bob and/or members of his staff to attend their annual convention in Cincinnati.

On that cold and dreary morning, with me riding shotgun with Col. Knox, ice began gathering on the starboard wing. The Colonel said it was all right, but pantomimed that I not mention it to the others. Since then I learned that the design of the airplane was slowly but surely being reconfigured as we gathered more ice on the wing. Not to worry; at 4000 feet it was clear as a bell and the ice disappeared. Another victory for Bob's good personal relations in Cincinnati.

On another formal occasion, the 25th anniversary of his company, held at the Sportsman's Lodge in Studio City, I kidded him with more fact than fiction: "Bob only keeps me around to call for taxis in New York City at 2:00 a.m. and buy Camels in Seattle at 4:00." I then gave a short speech about dignity that really was quite moving, because no one who ever dealt with Bob came away without feeling better about himself, more important, more meaningful, more fulfilled, more wanted, more dignified. And his treatment of others was exactly the same, whether they were dishwashers or the CEO of Coca Cola.

Conversely, on another occasion, at the Mayflower Hotel in Washington, DC, I learned the hard way that you don't put down or embarrass someone in front of others. After a long night, four or five of us were in the parlor of the suite talking, but mostly listening to a couple of the restaurant guys. Colonel Knox volunteered a suggestion regarding food service. I piped up with something like, "Let them handle it, Colonel." Bob, who was eating his usual crackers and milk, motioned me to one of the bedrooms. I got ready for bed and crawled in, only to have Bob come in, sit on the edge of the other bed, and say, "You're through!" Not knowing what he meant, I said, "Sure, Bob." Bob pressed on by saying, "You're finished." Wow, it finally hit me what happened. I had embarrassed Colonel Knox in front of others and was finished at Bob's. When we were walking out of the hotel lobby at

GEORGE, MICHAEL and ELLIS BOURY of Elby's Big Boy are shown with Bob Wian during one of his visits to the Ohio Valley. Elby's, as the sign indicates, is home of the Big Boy Hamburger. For a short time it was also home for the original Mr. Big Boy.

8:00 A.M., Tommy Holman told me that Bob had reconsidered.

Colonel Knox, trained in gliders and also a multi-mission DC-3 Burma Road pilot during World War II, was a low-key confident pro. Bob hired him when he purchased the 7-passenger twin-engine Aero Commander, "June Bug". Bob thought the world of E.P. and always made an extra effort to include him in our activities, but not tax his stamina. E. P. was always the first to go to his room after dinner if flying the next day. During a 17-day 10,000 mile trip around the country, visiting with franchisees (28 states, 46 cities), it became obvious that E. P. was getting a little bushed, not just from flying, but from the constant stress of flying a well-known figure and his executives to cities all over the country. In every case there would be radio, TV, or print interviews—even a parade or two, skywriters, keys to the city, you name it. The franchisees really put it on when Bob came to town. They all loved the guy, and it was mutual..

Making the rounds visiting the franchisees was hard work for Bob because of the media attention. While he was very cordial and accommodating to their needs, he was really more comfortable just visiting with the operators and their staff. The celebrity business, he thought, was somewhat overdone.

On a plane trip to Keane, New Hampshire, on a beautiful Saturday afternoon, to visit with franchisee Manfred Bernhard, creator of the Big Boy Comic Book, Bob got his comeuppance. As the plane prepared for the approach, the tower requested we come in from another direction, and as we passed over the field, we could see thousands of people and a band, all in a festive mood. Bob said, "Manny really went all out this time." Bob was seated in the back of the plane. Colonel Knox and I didn't mention to Bob what was going on, as he was in the process of straightening his tie and putting on his suit coat, finger-combing his hair and getting ready for another "really big show". When Colonel Knox approached the second time and landed on an isolated runway a quarter mile from the crowd, Bob said, "Do we have to walk all the way up there?" At the same time, Manfred greeted us at the plane in his car, loaded us in, and we drove in an opposite direction to his restaurant, Mr. "B's". Bob never said a word. I think he was a little disappointed. Certainly a humbling experience. Bob didn't know they were having their annual air show.

While the trip was going along quite well, E. P. Knox was showing the strain, and Bob became acutely aware of the situation in Minot, North Dakota, when the tower let Colonel Knox know that he had not dropped his wheels. Being quite close to the ground, Colonel Knox kicked the plane into high gear and started over. The taking off sensation before landing really bothered Bob. It was decision time, and he knew it. The pressure was just too much on Bob and E. P., keeping in mind that Bob was never reckless with the safety and welfare of his people, regardless of their station or stature. What to do? Bob called me aside after the landing and told me to find a co-pilot for E. P. We had only Denver and Provo left on the schedule. I found a pilot; we made it home safe and sound, sent the co-pilot home on a commercial flight, and parked the plane in our regular spot next to Howard Hughes' plane at Butler Aviation in Burbank. (Yes, it's true: Mr. Hughes had a 24-hour guard in the hangar taking care of a plane he never used.)

Bob had a real problem and it hurt him more than anyone knew. He had to let Colonel Knox go. But if you knew Bob Wian, you knew he would find a way to ease the hurt for E. P. and his wife, Dottie. He couldn't just fire Colonel Knox, but he could sell the plane. He sold the plane.

A few months later in Cabo San Lucas, Mexico, Colonel Knox, flying a converted Beechcraft H-18 for Thriftimart, a major food chain at the time, crashed on takeoff. On board were Bob Laverty and his wife, co-owner/operator of the supermarkets, the co-pilot and two others. The pilots and a Thriftimart employee died in the crash. Witnesses said that the pilot tried to step down the fall to the ground as glider pilots are trained to do when there's a loss of wind. It was also reported that the co-pilot might have taken over at the last moment because the step down technique stopped prior to contact with the ground. Colonel Knox knew the territory, having flown Bob and others many times to the Big Boy shrimp operations in Guymas and Mazatlan. They later discovered there was water in the fuel causing the engines to fail.

It was customary for suppliers to offer expensive gifts to key people, particularly during the holidays. Rather than accept or encourage others to accept the largesse, he set up a system where all gifts would be given as prizes at the annual Employee Turkey Trot on Thanksgiving and the annual Christmas on party Christmas Day, in addition to the Golf Tournaments.

The golf tournaments were attended by managers, supervisors, and executive staff, as well as representatives of each supplier: Coca Cola, Simplot, Dixie Cup, Heinz, Kraft, Behan Ice Cream, Patman Meats. Plumbers, air conditioning people, subcontractors, et al., also

Supervisors Don Fagan as Al Hirt & Carl Thornton, Harry Matthews, Bob Glassett and Bob Eakin as the Beatles.

Somebody won a new car...one of two.

...just a slight flirtation...

"WITH THE PERSONAL COMPLIMENTS OF BOB"

BOB WIAN 4th ANNUAL INVITATIONAL •
LaCosta Country Club • 26-27 April '66 •

attended. An added bonus for Bob's was the chance for store management and supervisory personnel to socialize with the top executives of the suppliers. They got to know each other and discuss solutions to problems for the benefit of all concerned. The only gift of substance I recall Bob accepting was a brand new black 1967 Mercedes Benz coupe. Len Dunagan was given a red one. The benefactor was Jim Behan, who had supplied Bob's with ice cream products for many years. Jim had sold his company and was out of the ice cream business when the gifts were made. You didn't bribe Bob Wian. It wasn't the thing to do. Your payoff to Bob was selling him a superior product at a fair price.

Bob's was closed two days each year, Thanksgiving and Christmas. Bob used these holidays as major employee relations vehicles. He put on first rate parties for his people. Count Basie, Les Brown, Freddie Martin, and Jerry Gray played for the Christmas affairs, and Bob gave away two new cars each year, in addition to the suppliers' gifts. The Christmas parties were always held at the best places: the Biltmore Hotel, the Hollywood Palladium, and the Beverly Hilton in Beverly Hills.

Bob wanted his people to know how much he appreciated them.

PROFITS

[BOB] "In high school the guy I most admired, Jim Steele, taught me all about bookkeeping—but not enough..

"I don't believe you can compete with profit as the only motive. The profit to me was incidental, in a way. It was the health of the business that was the most important thing, because with a healthy business you can always get the profits. Many times we would go through months of slack profits because of supplier price increases, but to introduce new people to our place, we kept our menu prices firm, while the competition increased theirs. We knew that once we got them as customers we could readjust for more profits. You can't do anything with profits if you don't have the sales."

If Bob Wian chose to multiply his millions, it would have been quite simple to formulate, but impossible to execute. Bob Wian had no desire to lose his investment in the goodwill and trust he had earned from his customers, employees and associates. His first boss, White Log Coffee Shop originator Ken Bemis, said in Fortune Magazine, July 1937, "If I could make a million dollars I won't try very hard to make any more," and money was not particularly Bob's bill of fare either. Ego was. After all, you can usually buy dedication, loyalty and trust, but money can't buy self-esteem you earn by being very good at something that is not motivated by bottom line. Certainly, many of his original investors, and eventually stockholders, expected more black numbers than Bob created. They were businessmen. Bob was a restaurateur. They counted dollars. Bob counted satisfied customers. Rather than raise the price of his Big Boy hamburger when additional profits were needed for employee raises or expansion, he would simply change the number of beef patties per pound on the Big Boy. Instead of eight patties to the pound, he would make nine. In other words, he got four and a half Big Boys per pound of beef instead of four.

It would be erroneous to assume that Big Boy should have been as profit oriented as, let's say, McDonald's; it was impossible. Bob and the franchisees were restaurant people, food people. McDonald's were merchandising and marketing experts and ingenious public relations practitioners. But you can't prepare hot sandwiches in advance, put them in a drawer or on a rack, and expect a heck of a lot. Bob's and its Big Boy franchisees were the "Unfactory." Everything was made to order and still is.

A couple of stories about Ray Kroc, the McDonald's franchisee, and the ultimate fast food giant. When Dick Ingham, at the time a Bob's Big Boy store manager, was helping Lou Frejlach with a new franchise in La Grange, Illinois, he was visited by Kroc. Kroc was impressed with the Frejlach Ice Cream Company's operation and offered Dick a job, an opportunity to "get in on the ground floor" at a new McDonald's he was building in Des Plaines, Illinois. There was, however,

78

a catch. Ray Kroc did not wholly own the franchise rights for Des Plaines; the Frejlach Brothers—Irv, Jim and Lou—did. Ray Kroc had purchased the rights from the McDonald Brothers, and the attorneys inserted in Kroc's contract that it included Cook County and the surrounding territory. I understand that Kroc, from that time forward, had a bad taste in his mouth for lawyers. The Frejlach Brothers stepped aside and got their franchise fee back rather than take a percentage of the sales. The Frejlachs had bought the franchise from the McDonald Brothers in San Bernardino, California. Would Lou Frejlach be a multi-millionaire if he had kept the percentage? Would Dick Ingham be a CEO of McDonald's? Not likely. Lou and Dick were food people, restaurateurs; Ray Kroc was a super salesman who made a ton of money and a lot of millionaires, and a new way of selling hamburgers, whether you liked them or not. (By the way, Ingham left Big Boy in pretty good shape, over $400,000 from the companies profit sharing program.)

Ray Kroc was not all bad. He once had a dance band. Bob Wian would have approved because he, Bob, was a whiz on a string base.

When McDonald's first presented and promoted the Big Mac in 1967-8, obviously a poor copy of the Big Boy, they produced a TV spot similar to one we had created. This was no big deal; it happens all the time. The unusual aspect of the copycat of product and presentation of a doubledeck cheeseburger was that they used the same voice-over actor that we had used a few months earlier. His name was Olin Soule (died February 1994), a very good actor and voice man in Los Angeles. You see, it was against AFTRA Guild Rules to use the same announcer for a similar product in a 12-month time frame.

Back to Lou Frejlach, one of Bob's all-time favorite people. Lou said in 1993,

> "After all is said and done, I feel that there are fundamentally two styles of management—leadership and dictatorship. Management by dictatorship will get people to comply with a directive, perhaps willingly, perhaps not. Management by leadership will create an atmosphere whereby people become committed to the task. Under Bob's leadership, people became committed. Everyday people from all walks of life came to feel important. They were important!

> "During some of our first meetings, several of us would gather and 'shoot the breeze,' so to speak. At times it seemed that Bob would dwell for long periods of time on some phase of the Big Boy operation, e.g., dishwashers; checking food that may have been left on the plates coming back to the dish-room; or maybe the importance of politeness between cooks and waitresses; the importance of inter-relationships with customers, children, suppliers, and each other.

> "We would discuss these items for hours on end. Then it dawned on us—Bob was drilling into us that in reality this was the Big Boy philosophy— the Big Boy success. Bob was saying: 'Hey, guys, it's not the bricks, building, or elaborate equipment; it's your people—your janitors, cooks, dishwashers, waitresses, cashiers, customers and suppliers.'"

Each year Coca Cola would buy twelve full-page ads in the Big Boy Comic Book which was created and perpetuated by Manfred Bernhard. Coca Cola paid a flat fee thought to be fair to both sides. Bob was not a chiseler, so when we met with Emslee Gault of Coca Cola to discuss the annual fee, Bob said, "just make it comparable to what Coca Cola is doing for Shoney's." Coke had recently paid a sum of money to Shoney's to help defray the cost of an elaborate exterior sign. Gault thought that was a fair proposition, and when the check came it was for $50,000, twice the previous amount for Big Boy Comic book advertising space. No one had mentioned a number; Bob only wanted to be treated in an equitable way. Suppliers were encouraged by example to be a good company to do business with.

COMPETITION

In the past 40 plus years Burger King, McDonald's, Wendy's, and Jack-in-the-Box have spent hundreds of millions advertising the fact that they can't make up their minds. They have had scores of different hamburger specialties and they are all good and well presented. Bob's Big Boy had one hamburger specialty in 65 years. Why?

The double deck hamburger created by Bob Wian has had hundreds of imitators, but none have been able to duplicate the uniqueness of the Big Boy recipe. Another reason is that Bob's Big Boy did not "float" their hamburgers as some others did and still do. That is, they do not make it in advance, then put it on a rack, in a drawer, under a heat lamp or beneath the grill. At Bob's Big Boy, you ordered, they made it... You got it fresh and hot.

If an extraterrestial suddenly became exposed to most fast food advertising, public relations and packaging hype, he might eat the packaging and throw away the food. As we all know, sometimes there is not a great deal of difference.

Ben Marcus, Bob Wian, Gene Kilburg and Lou Frejlach.
Some franchisees and the franchisor get together.

ADVERTISING AND MERCHANDISING

When Bob's Big Boy was formulating an advertising campaign, two things had to be considered. One, do we need it? And, two, are the restaurants operating at their very best? If for some reason one of the units was having a problem, such as a recent shift in managers, a still-to-be completed construction addition, or an exterior or interior decorating project, the advertising was called off. Bob didn't feel comfortable advertising excellence unless he could provide it, and that's how he built a business using the most effective advertising ever known, word of mouth. On the other hand, not just once, but many times, a single customer complaint would totally dominate the marketing strategy for the company.

We shot a hilarious 60-second commercial featuring Arte Johnson of "Laugh In" fame. Arte danced on the restaurant counter, holding a Big Boy hamburger, singing "Just get a Big Boy, a delicious Big Boy, and fill your heart with joy." Two of Bob's customers called and complained to supervisor Bob Eakin about an actor dancing on the counter of their favorite Big Boy restaurant. I pulled the spot. Later, Bob told me I had made a mistake. It was a great commercial.

The advertising program for 1966 and 1967 was the best restaurant advertising in the country. Full-page, full-color ads in Look, Life and Sunday supplements, painted and paper outdoor boards, 60, 20 and 10-second TV spots and scores of radio commercials. Grey Advertising was the agency, and they did some outstanding work. Their client frequently frustrated them, however, as Bob and I had our own ideas and encouraged the agency to use them. The Account Executive was Joe Waters, who later became CEO of Princess Cruise Lines, Cunard, and now Crystal Cruises. One of the people who created many of the radio commercials was comedian Bob "Super Dave Osborne" Einstein. Bob was the son of a very famous comic of the 30's and 40's, Parkyakarkas, and is the brother of writer-actor, Albert Brooks.

Other very talented people who appeared in Big Boy advertising included Joe "Captain Binghampton" Flynn of McHale's Navy, Joyce Jameson, and Jack Bailey of "Queen for a Day." Franchisees in most cases had their own agency and used, quite satisfactorily, Jonathan Winters, Flip Wilson, Soupy Sales, Jimmy Durante, Chick Hearn, Joan Rivers, and Johnny Bench.

Prior to the appointment of Grey, the advertising was "in-house," serviced by Ads and Associates, an agency with offices in Toluca Lake. Down the hall was Gene Autry's private office . . . a very sober gentleman even when dead drunk. Bob's oldest son Bobby was part of the team, along with superb graphic artists like Bill Webb and Frank Hubbard. Bill was the artist for the now-famous Bob's Big Boy poster. Frank created many of the advertisements on these pages. Every award worth getting was given to Bob's for their advertising.

Today the competition in the West is more in marketing techniques than food and service. Bob Wian would not appear in television spots, but Carl's Jr.'s Carl Karcher was very effective.

A really great on-camera merchandiser was Dave Thomas, founder of Wendy's. Alex Azar, longtime Big Boy operator and owner of five hotels including two Marriott's recalls selling lunchmeat to a hungry Dave Thomas when Dave was resident of the local YMCA. Orphan Dave

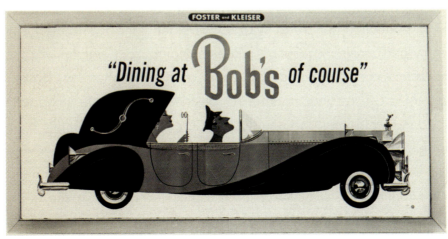

was 16 and Alex, just back from WW II, owned the grocery. They became good friends until Dave's death January 8, 2002.

Quick story: Later Dave worked for Kentucky Fried Chicken honcho, former Kentucky Governor John Brown...husband of Phyllis George. Thomas and Brown agreed to disagree and Dave, unsophisticated, uneducated, lacking in good verbal skills, did well anyway because he owned a good chunk of KFC stock and got top dollar from Brown to agree to a buyout. Way to go Dave!

Bob did appear in a Look Magazine full-color, full-page ad for a franchisee. Their advertising agency hired one of the country's best photographers to shoot the Wian picture in Los Angeles, for stripping in later. We got to the studio at 9:00 a.m., and 67 shots later, at 11:30 a.m., we finished. Now, two and a half hours under the lights doing something he really did not want to do produced what you might expect—lousy pictures. Toward the latter part of the shoot,

Bob's cheeks looked like his famous Half Pound of Ground Round...before it was put on the grill.

In Southern California, Denny's, Jack In the Box, Taco Bell, the pizza outlets, Tommy's, In 'N Out (On 6-1-02 L.A. Time's Marc Ballon reports 164 units, annual sales $263 million, $1.6 million per store). Marie Callender's and Hamburger Hamlet all have unique and very persuasive marketing strategies. Hamburger Hamlet was the first to market a gourmet hamburger in a comparatively elegant atmosphere. At Harry Snyder's first In 'N Out in 1948, a drive-thru hamburger business, they tissue wrapped and bagged their burgers to maintain heat and neatness, an idea created originally by Bob's Big Boy 10 years earlier. Son Rick who took over for his dad, died with others when their small plane crashed in Long Beach, California, due to a vacuum created by a Boeing 747. Mrs. Snyder, Harry's mother, is still active in the business even though she is in her eighties. They do a terrific job serving the public.

Dinner for 4. Less than $5.

We're getting to be a family habit. And for more than one reason. Jumbo shrimp fresh from the Gulf and our Chef's Special Salad Bowl are just two delicious examples. Also, there's the Big Boy Combination Plate and Ground Round Dinner made with freshly ground lean beef. Not to mention hearts of chilled lettuce, mounds of french fries, and toasted buttered buns. All this and beverages too for less than $5. Maybe that's why more people are endorsing the Home of the Big Boy as a habit worth keeping.

Shoney's Family Restaurants

V.I.P. treatment all the way... at the Home of the Big Boy

It's our way of making your family dining relaxed and enjoyable. Good wholesome food, modestly priced is only the start. Our staff is trained to take the wait out of waiting. We take special pride in adding that extra touch that makes you feel like a guest, not a customer. It's a friendly place. Drop in. Relax. Stay for dinner, the V.I.P. treatment is on us.

Ken's Family Restaurants

National Big Boy Advertising Campaign, '66 & '67
Look Magazine, Reader's Digest, Supplements

Everything fresh, fresh, fresh at the Home of the Big Boy

It's a case of using only fresh, choice ingredients. Like freshly-ground tender lean beef. Farm-fresh Idaho potatoes and sweet Bermuda onions. Only crisp hearts of lettuce and vine-fresh tomatoes go into our chilled salads. At the Home of the Big Boy, quality and freshness make the difference. Drop in. Stay for dinner. Let us prove our point.

Shoney's Family Restaurants

Cut out this coin

Get 1 FREE BIG BOY – when you buy one!

We're celebrating the 30th Anniversary of the Big Boy with a special. It's our way of thanking our many customers and introducing new ones to the Big Boy. The original double deck hamburger that made us famous. Just cut out the coin and bring it to any one of the Big Boy restaurants listed below. You'll get a free Big Boy when you buy one at the regular price. Treat a friend or enjoy the second one on us. Look for the Big Boy in the red and white checked pants. That's the place.

Bob's Family Restaurants

AAW Award Winners

Tommy's Original World Famous Hamburgers created by Tommy Koulax, a walk-up operation, has 18 stores and is particularly famous for the chili and tomato they add to their great tasting hamburger. Tommy's, frequently copied but never duplicated, half wraps the sandwich in tissue to keep the chili and the rest of the sandwich intact for eating and not spilling. Big Boy, until 1970, not only half-wrapped the Big Boy in tissue, but put it in a printed glassine bag. Marriott chose to forego the tissue wrap and bag for reasons that could only be bottom line considerations. The tissue wrap made the Big Boy manageable so that it fit snugly, but not tightly, in the Big Boy bag that graphically reminded the customers that they were indeed enjoying the original doubledeck hamburger. Rarely did the customer take the Big Boy out of the bag and remove the tissue wrap before the first few bites. It was a packaged deal. "Big Boy, Big Boy the Original Meal on a Bun."

One of the most effective advertising tools was the Big Boy Mobile Restaurant. This was simply a Big Boy Hamburger kitchen on wheels, designed for the promotion and sale of the Big Boy, French fries, soft drinks, coffee and tea.

The mobile was a franchise that Bob gave to me after other employees with more seniority approved. Originally, it was to test market new products, new territories, new concepts. Unfortunately, Bob left as owner/operator of Bob's Big Boy as the construction of the mobile was being completed, and it was seldom used as originally intended. It did, however, do a good job for Bob's Big Boy at fairs, conventions, horse shows, and golf tournaments. It cost $8,734 to build, of which Coca Cola paid $7,500 to market a new product, Fresca. They saw the potential and assisted in the construction cost. The out-of-pocket cost was $1,234. The $1,234 investment eventually earned $250,000, although never used more than 65 days a year. None of the other franchises used the concept due to the logistics and other considerations, but it was certainly a winner. After all, the customers got the Big Boy hamburger in their hands within five or ten seconds after it was prepared. But the enterprise would have brought two or three times that figure if the Marriott hierarchy had been more helpful in the operation and sale of the Big Boy Mobile Restaurants. Simply put, after Bob Wian left the company, jealousy reigned supreme that an advertising guy was so successful in selling and publicizing the Original Double-Deck Big Boy.

In September of 1971, the Big Boy Double-Deck Hamburger was entered for judging at the California State Fair and Exposition at Sacramento. While there were no Big Boy Restaurants within 400 miles of Sacramento, it was thought that Big Boy would score well with the judges. Big Boy whiz Joe Gutierrez transported the Bob's Mobile Big Boy to the fair site and prepared 1200 Big Boys for judging over a seven-day period. The Fair people quartered the Big Boys to get opinions from their "Consumer Reaction Program." Big Boy, the Original Doubledeck Hamburger, received a Gold Medal Award for Excellence, with a 99.52% approval rating, the highest in the Fair's 25-year Consumer Reaction Gold Medal Program. One or two people didn't like the red relish.

BOB'S BIG BOY

GOLD MEDAL WINNER
FOR PRODUCT EXCELLENCE
CALIFORNIA STATE FAIR
CONSUMER REACTION COUNCIL

SHOWCASE OF THE GOLDEN STATE
CALIFORNIA EXPOSITION

AWARDED TO
BIG BOY
FOR
BIG BOY DOUBLE DECKER
CHEESEBURGER
Consumer Reaction
Council
1971

BOB'S BIG BOY

MEDAL WINNER
PRODUCT EXCELLENCE
CALIFORNIA STATE FAIR
CONSUMER REACTION COUNCIL

we're happy you're visiting us....
AND HOPE YOU'LL ENJOY THE FOOD AND SERVICE WE OFFER

BOB'S BIG BOY

"It's A Boy" Firemen bring Big Boy back to life after kidnapping from fair site. Ventura Historical Museum

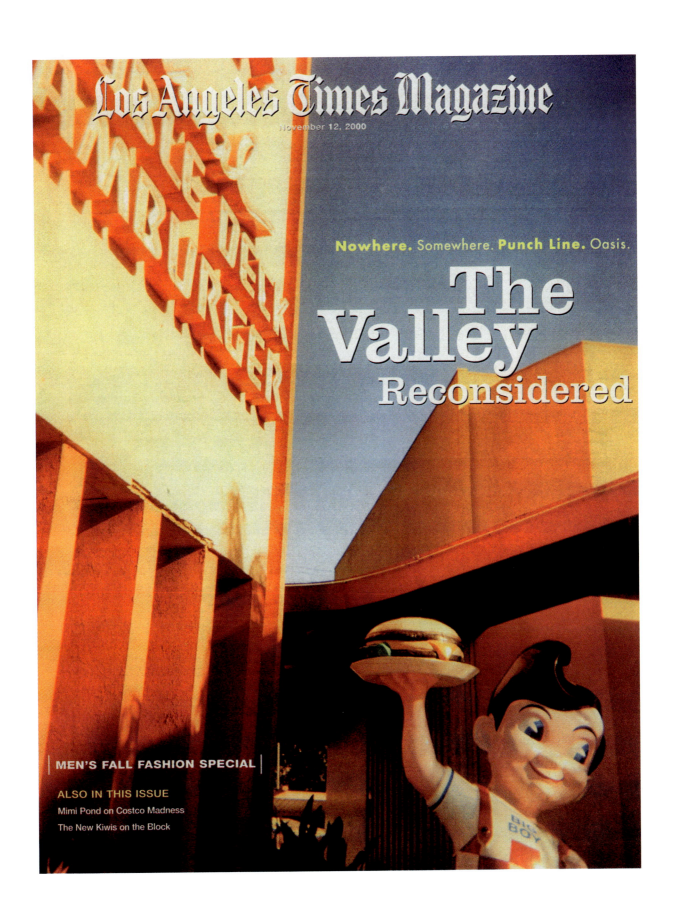

★ HOORAY ★ FOR HOLLYWOOD

Left: Bob "Super Dave Osborne" Einstein, writer Big Boy radio commercials & Chris Hansen;

Right: Chris Hansen accepts Maxim Award from Sterling Rinear.

Above right: Superstar Mike Myers and Big Boy Int'l Honcho Tony Michaels.

Above left: The one and only Jonathon Winters.

Top left: Three Stooges and gorgeous girl Lola Hansen, wife of 55 years of "King of Them All" author.

★ Top right: Comedian fashion guru Joan Rivers with Big Boy's Roy Raskin. ★

CITY IN TORMENT!

PHOTOS BY AARON MAYES / LAS VEGAS SUN

Shocked, anguished and wracked with fear,
Las Vegas weeps and wonders through its tears:

What happened to Big Boy?

GAGS, GAMBLING, BOOZE, AND BUDDIES

Bob, with his insatiable appetite for life, could be a mischief maker. Corny, practical joker, funny, and fun. One of the boys. He would stop at nothing for a laugh or at least a laugh for others. He was kind of a set-up guy, who would then stand on the sidelines, completely innocent of any questionable behavior. Some management studies stress that a top management with a sense of humor directly enhances job performance. In Bob Wian's case it probably made his productivity more palatable. If you didn't like to laugh a lot, especially during social occasions, you were working for the wrong guy.

On one occasion he rented an elephant from Jungleland in Thousand Oaks, northwest of Los Angeles, which at the time catered to the motion picture and television industry. To recognize his buddy Bill Barkoff on his birthday, he arranged to have the elephant taken to Barkoff's house in Toluca Lake. The trainer had been instructed to say, when the maid answered the door, that it was a gift from Barkoff's wife, Faye, and to lead the elephant into the house. The maid, not particularly fluent in English, cooperated, to the dismay of Bill and Faye. Not that the elephant didn't have good manners, but when he walked through the kitchen, he swished his tail and knocked the knobs off all the cabinets and drawers not to mention the trays of hors d'oeuvres and other goodies just prepared for the party. The elephant ran the caterers out of the house and down the street. Faye's well-planned party for husband Bill was not the social event of the year. It was smashing, yes, but not a success. The elephant was last seen walking down Moorpark Street past Bob Hope's house en route to Lakeside Golf Club. A donkey would have caused less damage, but Bob being a Republican wanted to be politically correct.

During an annual Big Boy Golf Tournament at Crystalaire Country Club in the high desert country north of Los Angeles, he bet Purchasing Agent Larry Kunz that he couldn't get the store managers to strip naked and march around the pool. A dare was all it took. Within an hour 40 of Bob's best people were seen marching around the pool, each with a bottle of beer in one hand and the other hand making a feeble attempt to keep ones self-respect intact. Bob was nowhere to be found, but the fellows will never forget the march around the pool at midnight in the warm desert air.

And that was the point: it was something to remember. He once said to a group of sleepy-eyed executives at 3:00 a.m., "The reason you guys stay up half the night is because you're afraid you'll miss something." And Bob was the type to make things happen that you didn't want to miss.

Bob was known to make an occasional wager, whether it was bridge, gin, high stakes dice, whatever.

Once on a trip on the Double Eagle to the Caribbean with stops at Mazatlan, Puerto

Vallarta, Acapulco, and through the Panama Canal, Bob, guests and crew became less than fun to be around due to limited bathing facilities on the boat. When they finally reached Aruba after almost a week at sea, the body odors were getting a little rich. Aruba, off the coast of Venezuela, did not know anything about the Double Eagle and its passengers, nor did they care. After a great deal of negotiating, they finally found a berth. They wanted to get off the boat and get cleaned up. When they found a hotel and started to register, Bob saw a sign "Casino." To hell with the bath, clean clothes, shave and a haircut; it was full speed ahead to the tables. Surprise. It didn't open until 5:00 p.m., and it was only 4:30. Bob decided to wait while the others checked in and cleaned up.

When the casino finally opened, Bob asked for his usual $5,000 credit. They refused, so he asked that they contact Las Vegas to check him out. They agreed, but Bob insisted that they give him $1,000 to get started. Fourteen hours later, Bob was out $17,000, and the only thing about him that was really clean was his wallet.

The next day, after a six-hour sail to Curacao, the Double Eagle was magically guided into a beautiful slip with all the pomp and circumstance of a visiting man of war. Two limousines were waiting on the dock, and it wasn't until the entourage got to the hotel and was experiencing all of the perks normally given to high rollers in Las Vegas that they got the message. The message was, "May I show you to the gaming area?" It didn't take Bob so long this time. He won back the $17,000, plus $7,000, quit while he was ahead, and headed back to the Double Eagle in a taxi.

Las Vegas

A city whose success is built on failure . . . yours. Mean, immoral, slick . . but just walking through the fabulous lobbies and casinos of the big hotels is worth the trip. An experience that may be worth a few minutes at the games of no chance.

[BOB] "Do people worry about what they've lost? It's a psychological barrier that you can't overcome. There was a guy goes up there with $100 to spend. Okay. Blows the hundred. Then he blows $500 more, full well knowing that it's an after-tax loss, and he has to re-mortgage his house or sell his stuff. There's no way you can beat it. Worried money never earned a nickel...just won't. I remember the time I won big time in Vegas and didn't know what to do with the money. Knowing June I hid it all over the house. I don't know if I ever found it all. I had two bags of silver dollars in the trunk of John Barringer's car for a month or so, I guess. That's harder to hide than currency.

"I think the funniest story about me in Las Vegas was when we were on our way to Phoenix, and I wasn't going to do any gambling. Manfred and E. P. both got stuck. So I determined I was going to get their money back. I walked up to the crap table, and the dice never stopped rolling. So I paid off their debt, which, between them, was around $1,200, more than either of them could afford to lose.

"As the chips gathered, I'd just give 'em to them and say, 'Go pick up your due bills.' So when they came back and said, 'We're all square,' the dice were still rolling, so when this one kid stopped rolling, I had about $21,000. Now that's two stacks of $100 bills about that high, you know. And I wouldn't take any due bills. I said, 'I want the loot.' So I went to bed. This was on a Friday. I didn't get much sleep, because you get emotionally involved in this thing. So I woke up and ordered a pitcher of Bloody Mary's and a pot of coffee and, by God, the guy comes in with it, and with him comes a sheriff. First time I'd ever seen an armed guard for a load of Bloody Mary's and coffee. I said, 'What's the gag?' He said, 'Well, Mister, I've been standing outside your door all night guarding this place.'

"It made a little sense. If somebody had seen me win that, they could have come up in the room, and it's enough money to interest somebody to do something.

"So, anyway, we flew home that day, and I went to Lakeside and put the money in the club safe, because I couldn't take it home. June didn't know I had gone to Vegas. I was supposed to be in Phoenix. What do you do with that much stuff?

"So finally on Sunday morning, I got the courage to tell her, on the pretext that I'd split it with her. She was still mad, so I went over and picked up the money. Sunday night the club safe was robbed. Somebody knew, but they didn't know I had picked it up Sunday [morning]. They thought I'd pick it up Monday and take it to the bank.

"I don't know what causes people to gamble. It's not boredom. I know I'm not as excited about gambling as I used to be, but it is really exciting if you win and emotionally disturbing if you lose. It arouses one's emotions."

Bob's first wife Frances, Bobby Jr.'s mother, was against everything Bob was for. They lived at one time on Glenoaks Blvd., just off Verdugo Road in Glendale. Bob, full of ambition, was bigger than life all his life. Frances was perfectly satisfied to have a less hectic lifestyle, stay out of the public eye, and just be wife and mother. At one time Bob wanted to build a big new home on two lots. She wanted him to buy one lot and build a small house. And so it went. Whether it is cars, houses, boats, Big Boy expansion, you name it. That's what caused the breakup. They were so different in their wants and desires.

[BOB] "Funniest thing that ever happened to me in Las Vegas, and I'll never forget it. I borrowed $25 from my boss and drove to Las Vegas to marry Frances. I had about $12 left...so I went up to a table like a big man and plunked down a silver dollar. I'd never rolled crap before. Frances saw that dollar on the table, came up and grabbed it and walked out the door. I was so damned mad we argued all the way home. Here we were on our honeymoon, you know, but Las Vegas is... I learned some lessons." "Vegas, there's no way you can win. You know they assault your ego. You get up there and if you're a wheeler-dealer, first thing you know you've got martinis right on the table and a big black cigar, and all of a sudden you think you can afford both of them, and you really can't. Then when you lose, the realization strikes you that it's after taxes, and you can't deduct it. Well, you're supposed to, if they offset your losses, but who ever gets in that position? Maybe Nick the Greek did or something, but I never did.

"Gambling. You can learn more about a person's character in a poker game than in any other way, and gambling is, well, almost all of life is a gamble, you know.

"Well, you've got to maintain your cool, whether you win or lose, you know. You can't have it affect you, so to speak. And it's exciting, like a drag race track. But I can't take the emotional strain any more, because I don't want to lose, because when I lose, there's really no way to get it back. But I've had some thrilling moments up there."

"This young kid that had this hot roll, he must have been 22 or something, he was playing with dollars, and I guess he made about $90, held the dice for about 25 minutes, and if you get lucky on a crap table and you're betting big money, it comes in so fast, you can't stack it, you know, because you get the odds going for you; every time you roll the dice, you pick up $600. So I had $100 chips, the whole rail wide, when his stack went down. So I took a stack like this, after he crapped out—just over my hand—$100 chips, and said to the dealer, 'Give these to the boy.' So the next day, I'm down having a cocktail, and the pit boss comes up and said, 'Boy, you're nuts. You know how much you gave that guy?' I said, 'What makes you think that I'm a sucker? If it wasn't for that kid, I wouldn't have the $21,000, and his share was only 10% of the winnings.'.'

"That same night I gave an older lady $700 or $800, and I gave the pit guys, the guys who run the ring, I don't know how many large tips, but it was about a 9-hour deal, so there was all kinds of tips.

"Sometimes you can psyche yourself into winning. It seems you can talk to the dice at times. When you get that feeling, you usually win. A lot of people go to Las Vegas, really, I think, intending to lose, and invariably they will. You've got to go up there with money you can lose, but with a desire to win. And then you can spot unlucky crapshooters just by the expression on their faces. But if you see a guy who's really flipping them and banging them against the wall, if he is trying and loses, it's not nearly as bad as if some nut gets up there and, you know, doesn't really expect to win; it's an odd one...well, anyway, it's mighty exciting to play but a boring subject to talk about."

On one trip to the casinos Bob was losing big time and worked the entire night trying to recover. Our entire group went to bed except Bob and me. At 3:00 o'clock in the morning there was only one other person and myself rolling the dice. Half-asleep with my head resting on the crap table I seldom saw the result of each roll. Finally, Bob did recover all of his losses and more, and as he gathered his winnings he gave me fifteen $100 chips. I didn't keep them, but turned them in with Bob's. I never knew if I had been rude, stupid, or devious. Thinking back I probably didn't feel comfortable about it but at the same time wanted to impress the boss. People were always trying to impress Bob in every way possible.

[BOB] "Gambling on golf is another matter. It became unrealistic to win, because golf is such a difficult game.

"There's no element of luck to it. It's all ability, you know. That's the reason there's no such thing as a handicap at cards, because there's that element of luck, which there isn't on the golf course. You may get lucky with a putt, but most people that sink putts are damned good putters. But with me, if I sink a 4-footer, that's luck. Golf is something I just can't get that excited about. It's impossible for me to focus my whole concentration on that little white ball. And even the desire to win doesn't really help.

"I guess it's because I just don't have the desire to learn to play really well. Most of the people I play golf with are fast players. A guy that hovers over a shot and takes an hour to make a putt, I get so bored I usually walk off the green. I'm thinking of the next hole, because I've done so lousy on the last one.

"Funny thing. There was a little guy by the name of Micky Rockford. Big time talent agent at MCA. Real short, you know. With cowboy boots on he wouldn't be over five feet tall. You'd lose him in a sand trap. But he's very, very concentrated, so to speak. He can really zero in, like on a putt, and he'll stand there and figure. So one time I putted out, and I had a golf cart with a squeaky wheel. I'm way over on the other side of the green. Micky was lining up his putt and just as he gets ready to putt, I start the car/ qwauk, qwauk, qwauk'. Well, I knew he was looking at me, but I waited until I got clear over to the other side before I stopped. Micky just stood there glaring at me, just glaring, and everybody else got just hysterical about it. I acted real innocent and said, 'Oh, excuse me, Micky, what's wrong?' He said, 'You and that god-damned squawker!' You know he got so mad he blew a two-footer. But I did it purposely, to harass him, you know. Great guy, Micky Rockford."

There were, of course, the usual bandits and opportunists that inhabit every golf course. Lakeside Golf Club was, and is, famous for many things. It was built in 1924 and became firmly established in the 30's. It was located in North Hollywood and Burbank between Universal and Warner Brothers studios. Early members included Howard Hughes, Harold Lloyd, W. C. Fields, Bing Crosby, Richard Arlen, Bob Hope, Walter Brennan, Gene Autry, Harry Von Zell, Randolph Scott, and Oliver "Babe" Hardy; later were Forrest Tucker, Glen Campbell, Frankie Avalon, Gordon MacRae, Efraim Zimbalist, and Lonesome George Gobel.

Lakeside was Bob's hideout, very private, very secure, with a great bunch of guys who were not totally against booze, a few laughs, and gambling mixed in with a little business here and there. Gordon Uhri, who worked for one of Gene Autry's radio stations, KMPC, would check in his office at 9:00 a.m., work until 11:00 a.m., hit the Lakeside bar at 11:45, do several hours of business right there over drinks, and still make it home to the wife and kids by 7:00. He was very successful. Occasionally, a client would want to play Lakeside, and that was the hook; after all it did have a golf course. Yes, there was a little business thrown in, some of it being monkey business.

A brother of a famous movie star regularly engaged Bob on the golf course at $10 or $20 a hole, which, mysteriously and quite calculatedly, turned into $600 or $700 a hole by the end of the round. Bob usually lost to hustlers but did very well gambling with his friends if he was totally sober.

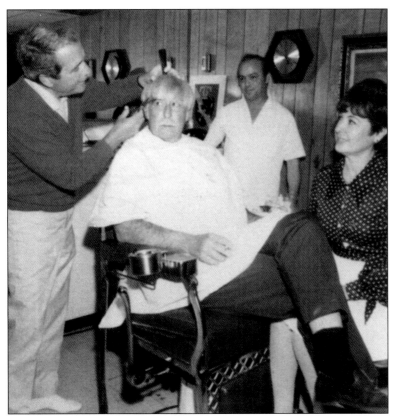

Lakeside Golf Club
Bob Wian wonders about former barber Perry Como's hairstyling technique.

Johnny "Tarzan" Weissmuller helps Big Boy hold up
Original Double Deck Hamburger.

Drink Vodka and Play Gin

One game in the Lakeside's card room, with two member hustlers, cost Bob over $25,000 in one night. Bob was playing gin and drinking vodka, and while rarely out of control, consumed more of the devil's punch than he could handle. Bob's good nature and good will toward others would not allow him to admit to himself that some of his buddies were absolute poison. Every club has its hangers-on, never-beens, freeloaders, sandbaggers, cheaters and scumbags. Lakeside had very few, but a few is too many. One member in particular was not looked on favorably by many members. They put together over $40,000 to buy him out of the club. He turned it down, even though memberships were only $12,000 at the time.

Johnny Weissmuller once said that he tried to help his pal Dean Martin, a very good golfer, by telling him that some hustlers at Riviera Country Club were taking him. Dean never spoke to him again. Successful people have too much ego to admit that they're targets; they just want to have fun.

A story from Norm Blackburn's 50th Anniversary Book on the Lakeside Golf Club as told by Bob Beban, long-time club member:

"One day after golf, a crap game started in the locker room, with all the contestants, naturally, on their knees talking prayerfully to those treacherous little cubes. A non-member named A. T. Jurgens, who owned half or more of Signal Hill [Oil], had the dice and was hotter than a pistol. I remember Dick Arlen [screen star] and Johnny "Tarzan" Weissmuller were two of the players, and the opening roll was $20. By the time I got out of the shower, the pot had gone to $2,500 and Jurgens wanted to have it all faded. His opposition by now was broke, so of course couldn't cover the bet. A. T. became angry, loud and insulting in spades, both to the players and to Lakeside. At this juncture, from around the next locker row emerged a rather tall, thin, black-haired man attired in long johns (complete with trap door in the rear). "You seem to want some action", he said. "You're damn right", A. T. snarled. "I always lose at everything when I come to this stupid club. Now I'm hot and nobody will cover my bet."

"Don't panic", said the thin man. "I'll cover it." Whereupon he called Phil, who at that time was major-domo of the locker room, and requested a blank check. He scribbled on it briefly and tossed it on the floor next to the $2,500.

"You're faded", he said, "and that check for $1,000,000 is good; my name is Howard Hughes. Roll the dice."

"Mr. Jurgens turned pale, gulped, and examined the check. You could hear a pin drop. Finally, without a word, he grabbed his $2,500

A MUSICIAN AT HEART

and made a fast exit. He has never come back. All parties involved hugged Howard and thanked him. It was really quite a moment. Lakeside had struck again!

Another famous flyer was Lakeside golfer and member, Amelia Earhart who lived on Valley Spring Lane bordering the club.

Bob would bet on anything. (Bob was 6'1", 210 pounds, with little flab, and had the build of a linebacker. You could hang powerlines on his legs. Famed wrestler Ed "Strangler" Lewis tried to talk Bob's dad into making Bob a professional wrestler.) Bob bet Hank Eschen that he could throw the golf ball around the course in less than 100 throws. The rules were very simple. Bob would throw, and when he reached the green he would add two strokes and pick up. First, of course, they loaded the carts with cocktails. It was about 4:00 p.m., and all other golfers on the course had already left the first tee as they started the match. Hank's bet with Bob was that Bob throwing the ball couldn't break 100, and if he did, he won the $100 and $100 for each throw under 100. Following the twosome in a parade of 14 golf carts were Bob's cronies, including "Circus Boy" producer Norm Blackburn, Dr. George Towne, Sports Historian Bob Beban, and many others. Bob had never broken 90 at Lakeside. He finished in the dark using the flashlights on the 17th and 18th holes. Bob was in considerable pain, as he threw out his shoulder and arm. Bob won the bet, but lost the full use of his right arm and shoulder for many weeks. He threw a 94 and picked up $700.

Shortly thereafter, Hank had Bob down $15,000 in a gin game when Bob uncharacteristically switched his beverage to black coffee. Hank should have quit while he was ahead. Bob got back the $15,000 and change. Play cards with Bob when there was no adult beverage around, and you lose.

The late Jack Swink, retired Superior Court Judge, ran the Probate Department for many years in Los Angeles and passed judgment on Cary Grant, J. Paul Getty, Howard Hughes, et al. Jack and I had been to Lakeside Country Club many years before when, in 1935, at age 10, we would go down to the Los Angeles River at Universal Studios, walk east toward Warner Brothers Pictures, run up the bank toward Lakeside's 12th hole, take off our jeans and tee-shirts and meander toward the Lakeside swimming pool at the opposite side of the Lakeside property.

Club personnel made sure we didn't make it all the way to the pool, but Jack did when he joined the club in the early 60's. An existing member offered me a paid membership in 1965 but turned it down because I thought Bob needed some place away from his employees. I was right at the time, but I'll be sorry to my dying day, knowing that I'll never have another chance to get into Lakeside—unless I bring a mower..

William Poklebekin, Russian author and connoisseur, said, "Vodka is a drink for gentlemen and only a true gentleman can drink Vodka while remaining totally sober."

When Bob bought the run-down, 50-year-old apple ranch in Julian, California, a little town northwest of San Diego, it was to get away from anything that reminded him of the

Marriott takeover. He did miss some of his friends, however, and on one occasion he invited the Bob's Big Boy District Manager in San Diego to bring his work clothes and help pick the apples. Promptly at 8:00 a.m., Bob, with basket in hand and a fifth of Smirnoff Vodka, proceeded to start the harvest. By noon, the vodka was half gone; however, enough was left for the afternoon pick. Dinner was to be spaghetti, which wife June had prepared and sent down to Julian from their Toluca Lake home. While Bob thawed the spaghetti sauce and cooked the spaghetti, a second bottle of vodka and a can of Dr. Pepper appeared.

The vodka disappeared by the time the spaghetti sauce was ready. Most of the Dr. Pepper was still in the can. At dinner a gallon of red wine was put on the table. Large water glasses of the grape completed the beverage consumption for the day and evening.

Let's see now, two bottles of vodka, at least a couple of liters of wine; there was, however, some consolation for the no booze set: he did take a couple of sips of the Dr. Pepper, and for dessert he ate a big bowl of Grape Nuts and milk.

There is more. On a trip flying over the Rockies, Col. Knox chose to go to 20,000 feet in the non-pressurized plane. Usually he would keep it at 12,000 - 14,000 feet. We all had oxygen at our fingertips and would just watch the altitude and put the little hose in the corner of our mouths as needed. Col. Knox could pick up a little favorable wind at 20,000 feet while Bob and John Barringer, our property development guy, did the right thing; I didn't. While I'm about to leave this earth, passed out, and going through the euphoria people talk about; Bob saw me slump over. E. P. dropped the plane while Bob and John got all the hoses that would reach into my mouth. It absolutely scared the hell out of Bob. When we landed, Bob had E. P. purchase an auxiliary oxygen tank, housed in a fancy carrying case, which was never used, except for one experiment on a later trip from Washington, DC, to Milwaukee.

The experiment called for a fifth of Canadian Club, a fifth of vodka, and the oxygen tank. Bob would drink the vodka, Tommy Holman would drink the Canadian Club, and after each drink they would chase it with oxygen, because they had read somewhere that the procedure would limit the degree of intoxication. By the time we got to Wisconsin, the alcohol was gone, and the experiment was going to be successful or a colossal failure. It was the latter.

Since they could not stand up straight in the cabin of the plane, there was no way to test their equilibrium. But when they got on the ground and straightened up, all bets were off. They could barely walk. Worse yet, our host in Milwaukee who met the plane on the tarmac had no idea what was going on. They staggered about like they were caught in a hurricane, trying to find their way to our hosts, the owners of the Milwaukee franchise and guests they had brought to the airport to greet the famous Big Boy creator, Bob Wian. As Bob and Tommy staggered, the hosts tried to make physical contact, but they were totally unsuccessful. Our hosts never knew the whole story. I wasn't going to tell them, and Col. Knox was diplomatically correct.

The only other time I saw Bob having difficulty from drinking took place at the Golden

Parrot in Washington, DC, in 1962, at an expensive and exclusive high-society restaurant. This was during a congressional investigation on whether enlistees should be given anti-Communist indoctrination before they enter the service, and there was a subcommittee probe on the issue of the military in politics that included testimony by Major General John Bruce Medaris, a handsome World War II military figure. He looked very much like Bob.

Regardless of whom Bob looked like to some, most people stopped what they were doing when he walked into a room. Very handsome, well-dressed, tall, white hair, a larger-than-military mustache, but always well trimmed. He never checked the room to see the reaction of the looky loos and lulus, yet he was always gracious and courteous without being patronizing. As reported previously, Bob had style and class like no one you've ever seen or known.

When the five of us went into the restaurant, there was an immediate speculation that Bob was General Medaris, which led to a lot of bowing and scraping in very plush surroundings. The restaurant's Captain escorted us to a very large, elegantly upholstered booth toward the rear of the room. Directly across, maybe 15 feet away, was a smaller booth in which was seated a lady of about 75 years of age. She was very slight, maybe a hundred pounds, beautifully dressed, white hair, expensive jewelry, and dining alone. Bob, while never a flirt, gave a soft, low bow to her as we sat down. The lady responded with a nod and smile. When the waiter came for the drink order, Bob said, "I'll have what she's having," motioning to the lady. The waiter took the rest of the order, which, except in the case of Col. Knox, was what Bob was having. It was called a Swirler, served in a large snifter glass. We learned it held one-half pint of 100-proof vodka. Hors d'oeuvres were served amid casual conversation, but the potency of the Swirlers was taking a toll on all of us. In the meantime, the old lady had ordered another, while fully enjoying an occasional flirtation with Bob. When Bob saw her well into her second drink, he said, "she's got to have a hollow leg." As dinner progressed, the drink took its toll. The first to go were two in our party, who were very intoxicated. Col. Knox offered to get them back to the Mayflower Hotel.

By this time, the old lady had finished her drink and had ordered a third, and so had Bob. I was still less than 20 percent through my first. Bob was beside himself that the old lady could handle so much liquor. As she prepared to leave, she and Bob exchanged a friendly smile and nod. They had enjoyed each other's company even from 15 feet. The captain arrived to help the lady from her booth, as she had some difficulty in getting up. The captain assisted, and as she arose, it was obvious that the old lady did indeed have only one real leg. Once on her feet, she was in full control, nodding again to Bob, and left under her own power. Bob was flabbergasted and said, "See, I told you she had a hollow leg."

We had been in the restaurant about three hours, and the booze had really gotten to Bob. When the captain approached and asked if the general enjoyed himself, Bob didn't comprehend the extent of the question. When I quietly told him that they thought he was General Medaris, he went along with it. It was time to go, but he was so inebriated that he tried to steady himself by holding on to the bottom of his suit coat. Consequently he had a robotic but very military look to his walk. While people thought he was being the super erect soldier, Bob was merely trying to hold onto something before he fell down. His shoulders were so far back that when he turned his head to the side he looked like he was walking towards you when he was really walking away. The parking attendant outside the front door asked where the general's car was, but I said, "We'll walk back to the hotel." The attendant, with feet together, bowed to Bob, and Bob gave a slow but deliberate salute. Bob was not so bad off that he couldn't enjoy a good gag. I found a cab around the corner. It was time for some milk and cookies.

Bob drank frequently but always in the company of his friends, and for 40 years I never saw Bob drink before 5:00 p.m. on workdays, nor drink heavily on consecutive days.

Bob had a lifetime bout with ulcers, one kidney and other aged illnesses. He wouldn't have been so hard on himself if he had had the ability to admit the pain to others and allow them to help alleviate or make the hurt less painful. Bob's problem was that he wouldn't allow others into his world and the stress of being bigger than life. That's how the drinking started: it was to ease the pain in his social environment. Yes, take a drink, ease the pain. Admit the pain; lose your bigger-than-life image. It was a philosophy that was full of barriers, and he ran right into most of them.

Bob with son Chappie about to tackle Lakeside.

Practice, Practice, Practice

Bob and Julie accompany crooner Casey (above); Bob on bass, Julie on guitar with CNN's Western Hemisphere Financial Correspondent Casey Wian.

Bob was always lucid, reachable and pleasant, except when playing "gut bucket bass" in his Clambake Five "band". It was his one consuming passion. Once started, nothing could get him away from the instrument. Bob couldn't carry a tune in a basket, and his sense of rhythm was highly suspect, but when he heard the musicians play, he somehow or other found a way to stretch those strings to a compatible beat with the music. On one occasion, Buddy Rogers, former trombone-playing bandleader and widower of Mary Pickford; Norm Larson, keyboard pro; Harry Cavanaugh; Wayne Mitchell; and Skipper Bob Sloan were on a Catalina Safari on the Double Eagle. Bob cooked all the meals on the boat and would normally start to prepare dinner when they were about five miles from Avalon. One of the reasons Bob prepared all the meals was simply that if somebody else did it or helped, the food wouldn't come out right in Bob's opinion, or, worse, somebody might get hurt. If Bob were going to leave the knife on edge as he did with Len Dunagan in the old days, he would be the cutter and the cuttee. Anyway, Buddy, Norm, Bob and the others making up the "Clambake Five" started to jam. Bob, completely engrossed in the music, knew he had to start dinner but couldn't tear himself away. Finally, Harry Cavanaugh got through to Bob that they had to get those giant russets in the oven if they were going to eat when Captain Sloan dropped anchor. Bob ignored the suggestion, and when Harry volunteered to put the potatoes in the oven, Bob, without missing a beat, said, "F... the potatoes." Dinner was a little late that night on the Double Eagle in Avalon Bay.

During one of our fishing trips for employees, a shift manager made conversation with the boss: "Big ocean out there," he said. Bob replied, "And that's only the top." The young man countered, "What are you thinking when you look at all that water, Bob?" Bob said with a grin, "What a chaser!" Vaudeville was back, if only for a moment.

MISFITS AND LOYALTY

There were no minorities at Bob's. Everyone was treated equally. Do your job, do it well, and don't interfere with the responsibilities of others.

> [BOB] "My thoughts may differ from others. They may come from a broader jurisdiction. I don't think anybody is born to fail; I don't think anybody is born bad; and with that in mind, you've just got to develop people and things will start percolating. It's a sincere awareness and fondness for people."

It was so difficult for Bob to let inferior people and associates go their own way, to fire them. It was compassion for others; he wanted others to be successful, but in many cases they were ill equipped or less than desirous of obtaining a better lifestyle. For Bob to let somebody go would take away an opportunity that Bob very badly wanted them to have.

Bob Hope, for many years, lent his good name to the Celebrity Golf Tournament held annually at March Air Force Base in Riverside, California. Lakeside's Maury Luxford created Celebrity Golf Tournaments. Somebody got to Bob Wian at Lakeside, and he ended up sponsoring the $25,000 telecast on L.A.'s Channel 5. The announcers included Dick Enberg and Keith Jackson, both real pros. Dick was to cover the 18th green, Keith the 17th. Bob Wian wasn't aware that Keith Jackson was on the broadcast team, but someone he wanted on the team was Bob Beban, a very good golfer, sports historian and, of course, a drinking buddy at Lakeside. Bob wanted Beban on the show to get some exposure, but there was only one place he could fit in the 17th. It had to be the only time Keith Jackson had been booted from a telecast. He was and still is one of the best, as is Dick Enberg, who also did the commercials for the show, a real class act who bent over backwards to do a good job. He did however make one mistake. His last line at the end of the show was, "We want to thank Bob Wian [which he pronounced wee-an rather than Y-N] and the Big Boy Restaurants for bringing you the 8th Annual Celebrity Golf Tournament." Dick Enberg was from Michigan. He didn't know how to pronounce Wian. Bob never said a word about it.

As I have previously mentioned, the company's Special Products Division manufactured a line of salad dressings and sauces sold in all the better supermarkets. They were exactly the same recipes used for the restaurants, and they were and still are very big sellers. The problem was that they didn't make any money. If the division netted $10,000 a year, the rationale was that they were good for advertising the restaurants and good public relations for the company. They didn't make any money, because the distributor was taking all the profit out of it. This went on for years. Bob didn't make a change, because he had given the account to someone he was emotionally unable to replace. But somebody else could do it? Right? Wrong. No, there had to be a legitimate reason to change. Nothing contrived, no fancy footwork, dignified. The opportunity came about when the distributor assumed Bob would approve a particular marketing strategy during a sales drive. It was a mistake to assume Bob would approve anything. When the unauthorized strategy took place, Bob called me on the phone and asked what I thought should be done. Because I was exposed to Specialty Products situations, it was a very simple job to draft a one-page outline to re-define objectives and how to accomplish them. When we started to discuss my recommendations, he stopped the discussion and said, "Take care of it."

Within 72 hours, a new broker, Bradshaw Wells, had been selected, the sales force had been trimmed, and Herb Hauswald had been hired as sales manager. We brought Herb over from The Frito Company, where he had had extensive experience in distribution and marketing research. Profits before the change were minus $9,000, and profits in 1967 were $121,000. Profits increased to over $500,000 annually in the early 1970's. Same products, but a different approach. Bob just couldn't bring himself to get rid of the distributor even though he was Bob's worst enemy in terms of performance. Most times Bob did not try to make a decent profit on what he sold. He should have.

During a business conference in Arizona with all the franchisees present, a public relations expert was less than professional in his presentation. The man was a new employee of Jim Mahoney, one of the country's best publicity and personal management people. Jim, who had as clients Frank Sinatra and other major celebrities, was shocked when I let the man go. Jim Mahoney doesn't lose accounts or clients he wants to keep, but when I explained to Jim the circumstances, nothing more was said. Bob had gotten the right decision, and nobody laid a glove on him.

There were many others who would find it difficult to find a job in most companies. One, a long-time department head, could barely read and write; another department head with one leg had a job that required a lot of walking. Still another put his hand in the cookie jar and got fired. Shortly after, the man and his wife pleaded with Bob to get his job back. Bob, having already filled the position, gave in, creating another assignment brokering the excess shrimp around the world. Part of the deal was that the fellow could collect brokerage fees from the excess. When the shrimp catches were less than good, the man sold most of the best shrimp to his personal customers, leaving Bob's with losses of over three million dollars in 1966 and 1967. Bob seldom struck out in his belief in his fellow man, but when he did, the consequences were personally catastrophic. He was not able to pass the buck or acknowledge that even Bob Wian was vulnerable to the slick and devious too often found in our social and business community.

Roy Raskin, certainly no misfit, had a decidedly unique background. A public relations pro (Max Factor Cosmetics), Roy learned his craft going to Los Angeles City College and Woodbury University while boxing as an amateur and training and managing fighters. He was California's youngest licensed fight manager at 21 years of age. Roy was hired to publicize the salad dressings and sauces to the grocery industry.

When the shrimp brokerage division (Leonard A. Dunagan Company) lost its sales manager, Bob got a fellow right out of the wild blue yonder, Bill Bryden, a former jet test pilot at Lockheed. Bill, not a particularly pleasant fellow, didn't know shrimp from Shinola. His favorite line when seeing you was "You look great; have you been sick?" Bill was a misfit, but at the time he needed a morale boost in the form of a job, which Bob provided. Bill's sarcasm finally got to him years later when he gave a former foreman's girlfriend a bad time at his fruit ranch in Valyermo. The boyfriend produced a shotgun and—enough said; but they never found the murder weapon or its owner..

Slain Man's Family Offers $10,000 for Information on 1984 Killings

Courts: Prosecutors hope reward will bolster case against Josif Jurcoane, who is accused of shooting two people.

By RICHARD FAUSSET
and JEAN GUCCIONE
TIMES STAFF WRITERS

The family of one of the victims in a 1984 double slaying has offered a $10,000 reward for information that could bolster the case against the man awaiting trial for the crime.

The suspect, 51-year-old Josif Jurcoane, was extradited from Mexico in April and charged with the shooting deaths of Lloyd "Bill" Bryden, 66, and his live-in girlfriend, Alice B. McCannel, 39. The slayings occurred July 4, 1984, at Bryden's Mountain Brook Ranch in Valyermo, near Palmdale.

Bryden's daughter, Nancy Roebuck, 55, said she and her two sib-

lings put up the reward.

"Since [Jurcoane] is incarcerated now, people might be more willing to come forward who weren't willing when he was still at large," said Roebuck, who lives in Palos Verdes.

Prosecutors are scrambling to bolster their case after an appellate court recently ruled that one of their key witnesses—Jurcoane's estranged wife, Susan—could not be forced to testify against her husband. The two have lived apart since he fled the county immediately after the killings.

Deputy Dist. Atty. Rouman Ebrahim said he has enough evidence to convict Jurcoane. "But it always helps to have more direct evidence," he said. "The reward is for any further information from anyone who can basically make it a stronger case."

According to police reports, Susan Jurcoane saw her husband grab a shotgun and shells and then drive off in his truck on the day of the slayings. After hearing three or

four shots, she told police, he returned and allegedly said, "Susan, I shot them."

Prosecutors said Jurcoane had worked as a farmhand for Bryden, but was fired and ordered to move off the property in late May 1984.

If convicted, Jurcoane faces up to life in prison without parole. Under an agreement with Mexican authorities, prosecutors agreed not to seek the death penalty in exchange for the suspect's extradition to the United States.

Jurcoane's lawyer, Arnold Notkoff, said the evidence against his client is circumstantial. "There's no fingerprints on a gun, no witnesses, no fingerprints on the cartridge shells they found," he said.

Since his April 27 arrest, Jurcoane has been held without bail at the North County Correctional Facility in Saugus. He is to be arraigned in Los Angeles County Superior Court in Lancaster on Dec. 12.

Anyone with information on the slayings is asked to call homicide detectives at (323) 890-5500.

Even those with a sexual preference that was not main-stream were productive and successful. One was a supervisor. Another, a shift manager, won first place in a national sandwich-making contest. He traveled the world as part of his prize, demonstrating his creativity. Unfortunately we were not able to capitalize, as the sandwich required ingredients not found in a Big Boy kitchen.

I left a lot to be desired in the attitude department. Bob put up with me because my job performance was to his liking. On a trip to Georgia, where the job was to massage a franchisee, I chose to let the operator know of his shortcomings. Bob was livid and later, as we rode the elevator to a fancy affair planned by our host, he was so angry at my bad manners he could not speak. He couldn't get rid of me then and there, and he couldn't skip the celebration.

As we reached the third floor, it was time to put on our happy face. Bob, so red in the face I thought he would burst, had to cool it. I finally said, "If you're not nice to me, I won't quit." It broke the ice. We both laughed, and all was forgotten. On more than one other occasion, I used the "If you're not nice to me, I won't quit" line, but it never worked as well as that rainy night in Georgia. Bob wanted his associates to succeed because he took a great deal of pride in making somebody out of a nobody. Bob protected everybody who worked for him, especially those who needed it most...and there were a lot of us.

Johnny Weissmuller was on the payroll for a year. Down on his luck, Johnny got a new car to drive and made personal appearances for Bob around the country. Around Los Angeles Johnny was not a big draw, but on the road, particularly in the South, he was very much a major star. Thousands would turn out to see Tarzan, and he never disappointed—with his famous yell, great smile, and presence—in what had to be a difficult time in his life. The pay was $1,000 a month plus expenses. He didn't like to be restricted too much, and while I liked him a great deal, I had to rein him in a few times. Imagine one of the world's true superstars in movies, as well as the Olympics, working for peanuts. Bob Wian never exploited Johnny, and when he asked him to let his hair turn white, because he thought it would add a new dimension to Johnny's career, Johnny refused. Bob never pressed the issue, and when Johnny left Big Boy to promote a biography of his life, Bob let him go with the dignity and respect he was always willing to give those less fortunate or down on their luck.

Bob's oldest son, Bobby, born December 3, 1937, was one of many on the payroll who possibly shouldn't have been there. For example, Bob Wian gave me two gifts, a 1-1/2 carat diamond ring he won in a gin game and a Stanford University football helmet signed by the famed quarterback Frankie Albert and other Stanford greats. Bobby Wian gave me a professionally mounted and bound letter from Voltaire to James Boswell with a note on his gold-embossed stationery saying, "Words can merely hint at what is in the soul"

Yes, they had different lifestyles. Bob smoked and drank; Bobby didn't. Bob drove expensive cars, had a yacht, airplane, club memberships, prestige, big house, beautiful family, a million friends, and a future. Bobby couldn't have enjoyed these luxuries even if they had been handed to him. He wasn't born with a silver spoon in his mouth. He was born prematurely with what became a debilitating disease in his brain.

Bob's dad, Pappy, was a catcher on the West Collingswood, New Jersey, baseball team, and Bob wanted a baseball player for a son or, better yet, a fullback. Bobby wanted to study at the Pasadena Playhouse. It was a touchy situation when young Bobby turned out to be less than athletic and competitive. In fact, Bobby's nickname by the other children was "Mouse." Bob resented this insult to his son's personality and character. They were not close until Bobby was diagnosed as having a brain tumor. Then and only then did Bob embrace the son he loved but did not understand. At least it was not too late. They had a loving relationship the last ten years of Bobby's life.

Bobby Wian did have one bad habit: he could spend money like a three-term politician. Travel, purchase of famous documents, letters, manuscripts, and gift giving. He could go through thousands of dollars in a matter of a few weeks. He could have been wealthy in the long-term, but he was always broke in the short. Bobby had a good excuse to enjoy life to the max, knowing his lifespan was going to be minimal.

These were some of the sad times for Bob. His first marriage, to Frances, Bobby's mother, ended in divorce. Frances was quite pretty and well-liked and occasionally helped Bob in his first restaurant by preparing the pancake mix in the morning and doing minor bookkeeping chores. Bobby, their only son, was a victim of retrogression due to a pituitary gland condition in the brain.

Bobby was probably the nicest young man you'd ever want to know, gracious, decent, loyal. He had a Victorian quality that endeared him to everyone. After one brain operation, he lost most of his sight, couldn't drive a car, was unable to read without a large magnifying glass held not more than an inch from his eyes and not more than three inches from the printed page. He nevertheless was the proofreader on all of our advertising and Big Boy Family News copy and never made a mistake in that capacity. He worked for Bob's for many years.

Even though increasingly disabled, he fell in love with and married an accomplished artist from Germany, Ingrid. The only reason they parted was Bobby's inability to help create a pregnancy. They remained very close until the end; Ingrid married again and has children. She still keeps in touch with the Wian family.

Bobby's condition continued to deteriorate to a point that, at 27 years of age, he was about 15 in appearance and actions. The last time I saw Bobby was at the UCLA Medical Center before his last operation and death in 1971. He was in good spirits, but was not optimistic for the future. He went through a hell worse than death. He was a handsome, highly intelligent, sweetheart of a guy.

We all loved Bobby, and when he was gone, we knew that no one could ever take his place. His dad never let us see his own hurt in him, but he saw the pain in us. We didn't have to discuss a tragedy we all lived with during the last years of Bobby's life.

Another thought about Bobby. Sure, he was the son of a celebrity and probably thought he had to live up to his father's success, but deep down Bobby was an intellectual who enjoyed literature, the finer things of life. He would not allow himself to be simply Robert C. Wian, Jr. He was born a hundred years too late and died 50 years too early.

Looking back I wish I had given Bobby a real hug—not one of those hugs where you put your arm around someone's shoulder and say, "How're you doing?" I'm talking about a two-arm hug that lets a person know you really care and are not afraid to show it. Bobby might have knocked me down for showing too much affection, but I wish I had been more demonstrative. It's too late to do it, but it is not too late to wish I had..

Others much less talented than Bobby became, over a long or short period of time, Bob's projects. These were people down on their luck or those who needed a career boost that people with power, like Bob, could provide.

Many of the misfits initially thought their job included dining at Bob's on the house, but if you didn't cook, you didn't eat—free, that is. Even though the administrative offices were right across the street from the No.1 Coffee Shop and Drive-In, non-restaurant personnel were not allowed to eat free or at a discount. In fact, no one was permitted to eat in the restaurant unless a sales ticket was written and paid for. The cooks and waitresses were not there to wait on freeloaders. It took some getting used to for the non-restaurant employees to learn the hard way that they were not welcome to pig out at Bob's expense. What a pity, they must have thought: all that food and not a bite to eat..

When Bob left as owner/operator in 1968, it was the beginning of the end for many of his most loyal, talented, and dedicated people. With Bob gone, many lost their desire to work for the new owners, Marriott. Bob's people felt the Marriott's were people who had tunnel vision, couldn't make a decision without a calculator, and had little desire to at least try to be the best. Was the Marriott Corporation a misfit for Big Boy? Apparently.

If they had given the care to Bob Wian's creation that they have always given to their hotels, there would be thousands of Big Boy restaurants around the country and we wouldn't have to look all over town for the perfect hamburger.

Staff Photo by RICHARD F. SWEARINGER

Richard Woodruff, who as a boy inspired restaurateur Bob Wian to name a new burger the "Big Boy," has died at age 54.

Bob's Big Boy model dead at 54

By RICHARD F. SWEARINGER
Staff Writer

Richard Woodruff, the man who served as the model for Bob's "Big Boy," the cheerful, chubby boy in baggy checkered pants, died at 54.

He passed away at North Hollywood Medical Center Monday after a long illness.

The figure has been the restaurant chain's trademark for almost 50 years.

As a child, Woodruff hung around founder Bob Wian's 10-seat diner at 900 E. Colorado St.

Wian called him "Big Boy" because he was large for his age.

"He used to go and clean out the ice cream machine and things," said Woodruff's brother Glen. "Bob Wian used to treat all the kids very well. His public relations were always real good. He gave him an allowance...and he even offered to put him through college."

As company legend has it, when he was 6 years old, Woodruff walked into the diner as Wian was trying to think of a name for the double-deck hamburger he had invented a few weeks before.

"Hello Big Boy," Wian said to Woodruff, and at that instant decided to name the burger the Big Boy.

According to Barbara Boyd, Glendale special collections librarian, Woodruff was also the model for the initial drawings of the Big Boy figure by cartoonist Benny Woshem, a schoolmate of Wian's at Glendale High School.

"Woodruff came in here about five years ago and his face, hair and expression were all the same as the Big Boy's," Boyd said.

BIG BOY: TOO BIG TO STAY SMALL

Franchising and Franchisees

After World War II, Bob Wian and his Big Boy Restaurants got the most sincere form of flattery: imitation. Fat Boy, Royal Boy, Country Boy, Goody Boy, just to mention a few. Copycats. Some did everything but call themselves "Bob's". One former employee, Tony Nevit, opened a restaurant two blocks from Bob's original Bob's Pantry. Tony called his place COPYCAT. Same menu design, double-deck hamburger, and most, if not all, of the food items. Bob could handle that by simply ignoring Tony, but when operators in the East began using the name "Big Boy", all bets were off. The Clock Restaurants in San Gabriel and elsewhere in southern California, owned and operated by Bob's good friend Forrest Smith, did not use the words big or boy to describe their hamburger specialty, choosing to call theirs Chubby the Champ. Many other fast-food friends of Bob did likewise. There were Big Boy restaurants in some parts of the country before the first franchise was awarded. A big problem was protection of the trademark "Big Boy". It was protected as a registered United States trademark, but to keep protection in force throughout the United States, usage had to take place. It was difficult to keep a U.S. trademark for a product, service or whatever that was doing business in one relatively small area of the country, southern California.

If you are not gifted as an innovator, there is another way to success. Beg, borrow or steal an idea, or better yet get the license or franchise from the originator. That's what franchising was all about, and Bob Wian was one of the first to use this concept to lend his good name and protect it at the same time.

What to do? Franchise or license the use of the Big Boy name in other parts of the country? Bob got lucky. The Elias Brothers—Fred, Lou and John—in Detroit applied and became the first official franchisees. Their headquarters were in Michigan. There was no franchise fee, but they paid a modest one percent of sales to Robert C. Wian Enterprises, Inc., to use the Big Boy logo. Because the Elias Brothers were already successful using their own name on the front door, there was no logical reason to use the name "Bob's". Furthermore, Bob preferred that all future franchisees use their existing name when they became part of the Big Boy family. There were reasons for this.

The main reason was the fact that the franchisees were not exactly Bob's Big Boy clones. They had their own way of doing things, and Bob was not about to get them to change. He respected and encouraged other people's success. In addition, Bob wanted to save the Bob's name for the Employee Franchise Program, the first of which opened in July 1955 in Phoenix, Arizona.

It has been said, and I agree, that when Bob allows the operators to use the mixture of mayonnaise and red relish (Thousand Island) dressing that the original recipe took a hit. It was true that the Thousand Island was faster but the texture and the taste were decidedly different plus the red relish oozing out of the top meat pattie added a lot of pizzazz to the sandwich.

What attracted Bob to the Elias Brothers in 1952 was their character and devotion to family. Their family was one of Bob's favorites, and Bob was more like a fourth brother than a business associate. In fact, Bob rarely looked at his associates as someone to do business with. He was attracted to their energy, integrity, stability and fellowship. They became good friends long before they became franchisees.

After the Elias Brothers came many others. Word had gotten around about the great success of the Big Boy concept, and in time most new franchisees used the Bob's Big Boy formula religiously, including design of building, menus, uniforms, the works. Even then Bob insisted that they call their restaurants by their own names or a coined name, such as "Top's" in Illinois, "Kip's" in Texas, "Eat and Park" in Pittsburgh; Marc's in Wisconsin was named after the late Ben Marcus, famous motion picture theater mogul and owner of the Pfister Hotel in Milwaukee; Elby's, after the Boury Brothers in Wheeling, West Virginia; Azar's after Alex and George Azar in Fort Wayne, Indiana; Shoney's in most of the South; Abdow's in Massachusetts; Frisch's in Ohio, Kentucky, Indiana, and Florida.

Of all of the Big Boy Franchise operators, Frisch's is probably the most successful, with 88 company owned restaurants plus 36 under franchise. They have been on the American Stock Exchange since 1963 and do an annual business of 160 million. They are also considered to be in the top 50 chains in the United States and employ more than 5,000 people.

In January of this year, according to the Cincinnati Business Courier, Frisch's Restaurants Inc. reached an agreement with Liggett Restaurant Enterprises LLC, giving Frisch irrevocable rights to ownership of the Big Boy trademark in Ohio, Kentucky, Indiana, and parts of Tennessee.

Liggett paid Frisch's a sum of $1,230,000, for which it acquired Frisch's rights in the states of Florida, Oklahoma, Texas and Kansas. Frisch's considered purchasing the entire package of Elias Brother's assets this fall, but concluded that it made more sense to guarantee and strengthen their presence in the core operating areas. Meanwhile, Frisch's has rolled out a new Big Boy restaurant design to focus on the small town market. The design will target smaller communities of no more that 25,000 residents, and will build on the Big Boy brand without cannibalizing existing Frisch's markets.

The design will feature a 24-foot high glass-block tower 8 feet in diameter, with a lighting system that changes the tower's colors at night. A prototype is now under construction in Batavia, Ohio.

Dave Frisch's brother Irv told me in the 60's that during World War II he had been in

Bob Wian, Oklahoma City Mayor Horrick

California Task Force

Mayor Horrick, Bob Wian, Bill Bemis

From left: Manfred Bernhard, Shorty &
Fred Bell, June Wian, Mayor Horrick,
Dottie Dunagan and Marti Bemis.

the Bob's Big Boy restaurant in Glendale, and thought the concept might be good for his brother Dave in Ohio. Dave was intrigued but short of funds at the time, put the idea on hold. Irv, better off financially, sent the train fare to his brother. But Dave, wanting to have a few dollars to spend during the trip, cashed in the train ticket and took the bus to California.

Unable to make contact with Bob, Dave returned to Ohio, where he designed his own version of the Big Boy character, a running Big Boy in blue striped pants and cap. Recipe wise he simply used an old family recipe of tartar sauce for the dressing and the rest is history. Family recipe? There's more. When Dave put the Big Boy name on the restaurant all hell broke loose because the crowds were enormous. A shocking development; so waitress Gert Davis really didn't know what sauce to use with this new creation called Big Boy. Mayonnaise, mustard, catsup, thousand island, what? Brainstorm; they did have a good supply of the tarter sauce they served with the fish entrees. You got it. Tarter sauce became the secret sauce on the Frisch Big Boy hamburger . . . believe it or not!

Seated: Jack & Blanche Maier, Bill & Marti Bemis, Dorothy & Ed Melton.
Standing: Bob & June Wian, Fred & Shorty Bell

Bob and Dave finally did get together, but it was to protect the Big Boys U.S. Registered Trademark more than otherwise. Another interesting ingredient to the story has to do with the speed of cooking. Frisch was attracted by the fact that two eighth-pound patties cook faster than one quarter-pound pattie. Faster food preparation meant more business and faster turnover for Dave Frisch and his restaurant, then called Mainliner.

Jack Maier was elected President and Chairman of the Board upon Dave Frisch's passing on February 10, 1990. Jack is now Chairman of the Board, and his son Craig is President.

But Bob was rarely disappointed in his judgment in approving an applicant to join the family. In all, through the 60's, in the more than 600 restaurants featuring the Big Boy, there was only one operator terminated because of substandard food and service, and only one restaurant closed due to lack of business. A phenomenal record and testimony to the excellence of the format and franchisee's dedication to properly embrace it.

In 1959, Texan Fred Bell had heard of and wanted a Big Boy franchise. Bob, who didn't know Fred, told secretary, Carol Monahan to discourage Bell and anybody else trying to obtain a franchise. Bell thought otherwise and proceeded to build a brand new, from-the-ground-up, coffee shop in Dallas using the same plans, menu, and uniforms of a Big

Settlement gives founder's son voice at Shoney's

Associated Press

NEW YORK — The son of Shoney's founder will get a strong voice in running the company as part of an agreement to drop his attempt to force out the chairman and replace the board of directors.

Raymond Schoenbaum and his allies will have three of Shoney's 11 board members and have veto power over a fourth. Schoenbaum and at least one supporter also will sit on a four-member board committee overseeing the day-to-day operations of the restaurant chain.

Schoenbaum said he wants to stop the company's strategy of providing big helpings of lower-priced food.

As part of the settlement, Schoenbaum agreed to drop plans for a shareholder meeting scheduled for next month to seek the ouster of C. Stephen Lynn as chairman and chief executive.

Left out of the talks was Ray Danner, a former chief executive and the company's biggest single shareholder with an 8.7 percent stake. Danner was surprised at news of the settlement but supportive of Schoenbaum.

"It Looks Pretty Serious."
Alex Schoenbaum, Ray Danner and Bob Wian

Boy restaurant. He did not, of course, have permission to use the Big Boy name, logo, or checkered pants statue. However, when he was ready to open, he again contacted Carol and demanded an audience with Bob. Upon learning the facts, Bob relented and awarded the franchise to Bell, giving all the necessary assistance with cooks, waitresses, and management. Bell opened as Kip's Big Boy.

Fred, tall with or without the boots, blond and handsome, and his gorgeous wife Shorty were superb representatives of the fast food industry in the Southwest, particularly if Bob and June were present. They did have great successes together, and more than a few laughs.

Example: Bob lost a bet to Fred on gross sales of one of Fred's new Kip's Big Boy Coffee Shops. Bob was optimistic, Fred more so. Fred demanded immediate payment, and

Bob obliged by agreeing to meet Fred in Guaymas, Mexico, with the money: $700. Fred, triumphant, met Bob at the airport as Big Boy pilot E. P. Knox helped Bob unload 70,000 pennies in canvas bags. (Bob was on the board with Baseball Hall of Famer Casey Stengel at the Valley National Bank in Toluca Lake.) In a separate, smaller bag were penny coin wrappers with instructions:

    1. Take one penny in your hand and check for authenticity.
    2. With your other hand take one coin wrapper, squeeze it open, and blow.
    3. Start stuffing.

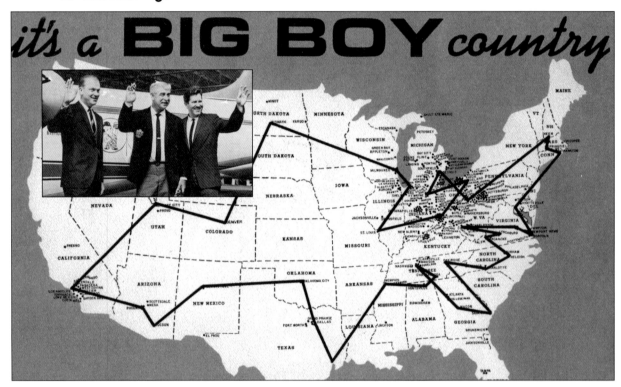

Bob lost that battle but won the war, as nothing seemed to bring more harmony and peace of mind to his demanding responsibilities than Mexican music, especially the slow stuff, the ballads. When Bob came home there was a Western Union paper telegram from Fred that said: "Dear Mr. Wian, Cheap Charlie you were short one penny, Mr. Bell."

The Boys of the N. B. B. A. were a bunch of wild and crazy guys who knew how to have fun . . . and earned it . . . We can't mention here how one became a member of the N. _._ A. but be assured the B. B. did not stand for Big Boy. Initiation was a bit bizarre, involving ladies of the night and an audience, and the really straight laced went through guilt city when being sworn in as a member of the National _ _ Association. Don't confuse the above with the formal National Big Boy Association that had principal Franchisees as Officers and Trustees. I was their Executive Secretary.

When I was with The Frito Company, one of our licensees was Herman Lay in Atlanta. Herman, a really sharp Princeton guy, eventually merged with Fritos to form Frito-Lay, then got together with Pepsi-Cola, where he became CEO of Pepsico. Having talked with Herman a few times at Frito meetings, I decided to go to his new headquarters in New York to present to him an idea of Bob's: would Pepsi-Cola be interested in getting into the food service business? Bob's offer was pretty simple. Pepsico could acquire the Big Boy name and expertise for all of Mexico and South America. Herman turned it down. I guess we were a little early with the idea. Later, of course, Pepsico acquired Pizza Hut and Taco Bell, and other large, non-food-service companies also got into the food service business.

Today, there are 314 Big Boy Restaurants in the U.S.A, 93 in Japan and 1 in Thailand. Numerous others are in the planning stage or under construction. On these pages are photographs of many of the franchisees.

Bob Wian's last physical work in Big Boy Restaurants was in the dish room as part of task forces opening new restaurants for franchisees. Dunagan, Fred Bell, and others spent many a shift in the dish-room washing dishes, preparing food, and teaching. These were not token efforts.

The objective was to open an operation as if it had been in business for a long time, so that no break-in, shakedown problems occurred. Complete crews, top cooks, waitresses and managers were flown in with the best Bob Wian had to offer, plus training films, literature, and enthusiasm. Once the franchise was well established, the task force was reduced, leaving the franchisee on his own. If, for some reason, a problem arose, task force members would return to help alleviate the problems. Occasionally a franchisee would ask Bob for permanent transfer of an employee. Ed Glassett went to Denver, Bert Borski went to Utah, and others went to other locations.

Once the franchisee expanded and had a labor pool to draw from, the borrowing of crewmember was reduced. Still, on occasion, well-established operators would bring in full crews, as cost was no object for the franchisee who wanted to be the best food service operator in the area.

And so it went. In the 60's, when the franchise operators should have come together, they didn't. Sure, things like menus, graphics, uniforms, and training methods did work, but few operators would invest their money in improving a national image via the media. Big Boy was lucky to get 1% for national marketing because most franchisees reserved their advertising dollars for local marketing strategies that were good for local business.

However, when McDonald's, Burger King, and Wendy's got up a full head of steam in the 70's, Big Boy knew it had a problem. A participant at our 1972 conference said, "The purpose of this conference was supposed to acquaint Big Boy operators with new plans for 1972. It's interesting that the people in charge did nothing. It's unbelievable that a company like Marriott Corporation—and we're at their Camelback Inn—can sponsor a meeting of this type, where the most important thing talked about to date is a Big Boy costume, a horrendous-looking Big Boy outfit that fits over the body of a small man." When Marriott took over the fabulous Camelback Inn the first thing to go was the shrimp at the noon buffet.

Bill Peters, then head of Eat'n Park in Pittsburgh, said it best during a cocktail party for franchisees at the Frisch estate in Cincinnati: "Buck Your Fuddy." (To that moment I had never even heard a darn from the very proper Bill Pitts from Petersburg). It was true: everybody was just out for themselves. We did, however, have a national marketing program that had superb food service advertising. Even then, some franchisees were reluctant to admit its value.

Alex Schoenbaum, of Shoney's, said he did not need or intend to use the national advertising materials that were provided by Bob Wian. He told me this while we were driving to Charleston, West Virginia, in 1965. At that moment the car radio was playing one of our commercials, and shortly we came upon a lighted outdoor billboard displaying our artwork and copy. Alex didn't say a word, and in all fairness his advertising people probably didn't tell him that national advertising materials were being used in the South.

Schoenbaum and Gene Kilburg, were in my opinion, the major obstacles to Big Boy becoming a bonified force nationally. Kilburg was the Ben Marcus' general manager. Both Alex and Gene were against a single image to identify their Big Boy operation. Alex, in fact, wanted to have Big Boy headquartered in Chicago rather than Glendale, California. Gene, in some of Marc's Big Boy units also served Kentucky Fried Chicken. Of all the franchisees, Alex and Gene were the most devious and unproductive from a national identity point of view. Alex died December 6, 1996, at the age of 81.

On the other hand all the guys for the most part were self-made. Schoenbaum was a three time All-American lineman at Ohio State. Fred Bell, (Fred and Shorty died in the crash of their airplane in 1977), with his Kip's of Texas, made his money running canteens at army bases. The Frejlachs were very successful in the ice cream business. The Abdow brothers were better known as football officials than as restaurateurs. Ben Marcus was the major motion picture theater operator in the Midwest and also owned the Phfister Hotel in Milwaukee. One time Alex Azar and I were sitting in a Fort Wayne coffee shop when lawyer F. Lee Bailey stopped to say hello. Alex let Bailey know that he thought his legal skills left a lot to be desired. Alex and Bailey smiled during a brief exchange till Bailey clammed up and walked away. Were the franchisees arrogant? Not really, just confident, especially when the Big Boy name at that time—the late 1960's—was without question, the most revered in the food service business.s.

Money, money, money. McDonald's, Burger King, Denny's, Jack-In-The-Box, Taco Bell, Carl's Jr., and Sambo's had plenty, and they knew what to do with it. At least 3% of sales went toward the purchase of print, radio and TV advertising and promotion.

The more we tried to unify, the less unified we became. The regional differences were magnified each time a program was offered on a national level. For example, in June of 1968 in Chicago I presented to the franchisees two network TV specials—Ann Margaret and Julie Andrews. Very affordable at less than a million each. Jimmy Parks, former NBC honcho who made the pitch, got nowhere. Simply put, many of the operators could not imagine the commercials without their logo on the screen. The Big Boy was not enough. It is understandable. Who ever heard of Joe's Jack-In-the-Box, Bill's Burger King, Tom's Taco Bell, et al. It is my contention, however, that McDonaldd's would never have advertised and promoted in 1993 the preposterous notion that they created the doubledeck hamburger in 1968 had the Big Boy family come together in the 60's. Even the Great Americans' Bicentennial Program I created in 1976 did not get full support by the franchisees. A series of trading cards and learning posters was very successful for Sunbeam, Rainbow, Holsum, and other bread companies. Eventually 30 million were distributed, but Big Boy, for whom it was designed, only received token participation by the franchise operators.

Many of the franchise operations had their own conventions. Frisch in particular was a close knit family, as were many others. Bob Wian did not really have his heart in a fully integrated, national image. After all, he was never in it for the money and was always aware that the others were and that their individual identity was very important to them, something to be protected. Another example of division came about after a National Big Boy Association Convention in New Orleans. Bob and others decided that the time and expense of big time conventions just wasn't worth it. Conventions well planned are a lot of work. Pick a city, choose a hotel, make travel arrangements, special menus for the luncheons and dinners, daytime entertainment for the wives, cocktail parties, new dresses, old tuxedos, speeches, awards, honored guests, keynote speaker, and, worst of all, who goes. Better yet, who does not have to go? With as many different factions as was the case with Big Boy franchisees, the conventions were not successful with the pooling of ideas for the common good. The franchisees were licensed to use the name Big Boy, but really, for most of the franchisees, the similarity ended right there. Therefore, conventions were merely a social gathering to promote good will toward each other rather than making long and short-term decisions that might create a stronger national presence for the Big Boy trademark and The Original Doubledeck Hamburger.

The national conventions had to go, but the question remained how best to change the

Photo: John Hogan

119

format and maintain some semblance of unity. It wasn't that tough. Bob simply changed the affairs to what he called "Executive Conference," to include the owners of the individual franchises, the real heavyweights. No wives, no dinner dances, no nonsense.

We held the Executive Conference each January at the Mountain Shadows Resort in Scottsdale, Arizona, with guest speakers like Roy Neal, NBC Space spokesman, and George Murphy, movie star of the 30's and 40's, who became a U.S. Senator from California. The wives did not like it. After all, most of them were from the East, and not being able to come to Arizona in the wintertime did not make for a happy household. The first two or three Executive Conferences went very well, but the good fellowship in the evening was non-existent, except for a few of us who were acting as hosts. The conferees would just disappear, and it was not until the final night of the fourth year that we found out why. (We did wonder if some of the fellows were trying to recapture their youth, but generally the conferees did not need to have their egos or anything else massaged.)

Jack Haller of Dixie Cup, at my request, sponsored a cocktail party at the hotel on the last evening for a final get together and social. Jack, Dixie, and the hotel really laid it on, with a 40-foot display of delectables that would have thrilled the most discriminating gour-

met. It was gorgeous to look at and delicious to eat. The invitations to the affair, both written and spoken, asked that the guests convene at 6:00 p.m. By 6:30, we knew we had a problem. Nobody came. The Dixie people, a couple of bachelors, Bob Wian, Manfred Bernhard, and I were the only people there. This was a spread for 35 men with normal appetites. It was a revolting development. We ate as much as we could, had some of the food sent to our rooms, prepared little wicker baskets of food to take with us, anything to lessen the embarrassment regarding Dixie. What in the world was going on? Where did everybody go? Where were our buddies when we needed them most? "Our buddies" were with their wives, who for three years had booked lodgings at Camelback, the Biltmore, and other posh hotels during the meetings unbeknownst to Bob, me, and the others. After all, they couldn't let on, because the wives who stayed home would have raised the roof had word gotten out. It was too embarrassing. Who could we tell?

The Official Publication of Big Boy Franchises, Inc.

THE BIG BOY FAMILY NEWS

SPRING 1967

**Schedule
Set for
Cross-Country
Tour**

In Memoriam
Services were conducted in the Church of the Recessional, Forest Lawn Memorial Park on Feb-

Big Boy & Marriott Merge

Robert C. Wian Enterprises, Inc. and Big Boy Properties,

deal. "We selected Washington because we'd heard it got

it was the last loan he had to make. Within two years, Mar-

The Official Publication of Big Boy Franchises, Inc.

THE BIG BOY FAMILY NEWS

1 9 6 7

MARRIOTT-WIAN UNITE

Woody Marriott (left), L.A. Mayor Sam Yorty and Bob Wian

Massive Food-Service Operation Formed

On Friday, May 26, documents were recorded in the executive offices of the Title Insurance and Trust Company, in Los Angeles, resulting in the completion of merger proceedings. Robert C. Wian, President of the Big Boy organization and Woodrow Marriott, Senior Vice President of Marriott-Hot Shoppes, Incorporated, signed documents making Big Boy Restaurants of America a division of Marriott.

The proceedings marked the formation of one of the world's largest food-service organizations. The new combination of Marriott-Wian and

MARRIOTT ABSORBS BIG BOY

J. Willard Marriott didn't want Big Boy nearly as much as they didn't want anybody else to get it. Bill Bemis, operator of Big Boy Restaurants in Prince George Plaza in Hyatsville and Rockville told me Marriott probably wouldn't pay more that six or seven hundred thousand for his franchise. I told Bill that they would pay a million plus. He laughed at the possibility. Naturally I countered with a proposition and told him they would give him a million and he said if that happens I guarantee I will give you a cut. Marriott paid the million . . . I'm still waiting for my cut. Maybe a gift certificate from Sak's or dinner for two at Mc Donald's . . . Christmas Card . . . postcard?

J. (J. is for John) Willard Marriott and Bob Wian had a lot in common. You know by now Bob's business career beginnings. J. Willard had a similar beginning when he bought an A&W Root Beer franchise for Washington, DC, rented half a bake shop, put up a partition, and opened the doors. That was May 20, 1927. Other than that, Bob had nothing in common with the rest of the members of the Marriott corporate family.

In the Marriott Annual Report of 1968-1969, Big Boy is well represented with photographs and other appropriate graphics and text. Ten years later in the 1979 Annual Report, there are ten Marriott businesses featured. Big Boy is not mentioned in print or picture. That's how long it took for the Marriott philosophy to begin the demise of the Big Boy.

On May 14, 1968, Bob left the company he had founded on August 6, 1936. He was then asked to take a seat on the Marriott Corporation board. He accepted, fantasizing that he might be of some help in Marriott's corporate objectives. He knew or had met most of the Board members:

> J. Willard Marriott, Chairman of the Board
> Jorge Bird, Legislator and Advisor on Tourist development, Puerto Rico
> Alice S. Marriott, Vice President
> Woodrow D. Marriott, Senior Vice President
> Don G. Mitchell, Chairman, Executive Committee, American Management Association
> Louis W. Prentiss, Major General, USA (ret.)
> Harry L. Vincent, Jr., Vice President, Booz, Allen & Hamilton, Inc.
> Robert C. Wian, Vice President

Now, for a former fry cook, this was a pretty heady bunch. High profile, well-connected, corporate pros, very definitely "inside the beltway". All very well educated, accomplished in their chosen fields, some professional board members. Easy money! It was a reasonably sound decision by the Marriott's to have Bob on the Board. It was good for the franchisees. Bob could be their mouthpiece. And good for the Marriott's if they knew how to massage an ego that was earned, not bought and paid for by others. If Bob didn't know their strategy, he should have. In their annual report of 1969, Bob is listed on the page with an asterisk (retired from the Board effective August 1969). Holy Mackerel, he just got there! I'll tell you what happened.

When I visited with Bob at his ranch in Valyermo, I asked him why he left the Board. His response was silence. I kept at him. "Bob, it was a good deal. Pick up a few dollars ($25,000); keep your foot in the door; it might lead to something." Bob looked toward me, raised his eyes with a look that did not invite more questions. His silence, however, created more curiosity, and I pressed on. "Gee, Bob, it's a reasonable question; you know it didn't make a whole lot of sense, especially in regard to your relationship with the franchisees." Bob, losing his patience, paused, not sure he wanted to tell me what I wanted to know, and said, "They never asked me any questions." That was his answer but a more complete response would have mentioned that J. Willard Marriott didn't like a pay scale that put Bob in a superior position while working part time. Simply put, the fact is they cut Bob's salary . . . twice. Snobs without portfolio? About as sincere and natural as hair on a biscuit? You can bet on it.

Bob should have known that at Marriott you had to be somebody to get to the top, but when they really got to know you stood for something you went to the bottom. Top of the heap to bottom of the pile. Bob knew more about human relations and the practice of serving and pleasing the public than all the Marriott Board members combined. And they didn't ask him any questions?

Bob had purchased a 20-acre apple farm in San Diego County and moved in. We were sitting in the living room of the 50-year-old frame house in Julian, California, which was in, at best, fair condition. The trees were older than the house. Bob pointed his finger at the front gate down a long winding driveway of about a thousand yards. Bob said, "Some day Bill Marriott is going to come up that driveway and ask me to help them out." I didn't look at Bob when I said, "It'll never happen." And it didn't. The Marriott's were not capable of asking for help, even if they knew of their shortcomings. They liked Bob, but they didn't respect him to the degree that he deserved. They were pencil pushers. Bob Wian planted the seedling for the tree to get the wood to make the pencil. He mined the carbon for the lead. He mixed the paint for the wood; he made the pencils, painted the pencils, packaged the pencils, sold the pencils, created a business for which pencils are used. You know what I and others wish the Marriott's would have done with their pencils.

> [BOB] "You can never lose your enthusiasm for what you're doing. When I lost it, I quit, because my people needed it; it's got to emanate from the top. It's best to get out of the saddle before you're shot out. I think timing is a crucial element in any person's success—timing at the beginning, timing at the end is positively everything.""

What has happened to the Marriott Corporation in some facets of the food service business is well documented. They have experienced some failures, and they didn't have the common sense to ask Bob Wian any questions? Bob Wian's power came from the people. Marriott power came from money.

[BOB] "Corporate development and corporate growth is incongruous in my philosophy, as you know. But I feel that anyone who is trying to grow in that direction should have the advantage of some persons, some person, who is not involved in the profitable, or the - what-

ever the growth program is, - so that he can sit down and say, What do you think about this?', and you say, Well, I don't think it's going to work", and you discuss it. So, anyway, I was abruptly, let's say— crossed out of the company, O.K.? because of a measly salary you wouldn't believe. It wasn't commensurate with the experience I thought I had in this business.""

Bill Marriott was not the only one who didn't see eye to eye with Bob regarding the development of Big Boy. Some of Bob's own board members in the mid-60's were putting the heat on Bob to change his operating philosophy. During a particularly stormy meeting in Glendale, board member Arnold Peterson let Bob know that the price of coffee in all of the principal competition was higher than in Bob's Big Boys, and an increase was warranted in light of the deficits due principally to the shrimp operation losses in 1966 and 67. Bob exploded at Arne, implying that if he or anyone else thought he knew better how to operate the company, they had better keep it to themselves. This was somewhat shocking considering the source. Arnie was responsible for Bob's having the site and resources to open his Big Boy restaurant in Burbank on San Fernando Road. They were great personal friends, whose loyalty and gratitude to each other was legend. It was one of those arguments where nobody won. One side just lost a little less. (Arnold Peterson was famous as the inventor and manufacturer of the Folda Rolla, the first collapsible baby stroller.)

Bob's job was on the line: merge, bring in a new CEO, or quit. With help or encour-

BIG BOY UNITS				JANUARY 1971
ALABAMA	11	KENTUCKY	29	OHIO	128
ARIZONA	10	LOUISIANA	3	OKLAHOMA	4
ARKANSAS	2	MARYLAND	7	PENNSYLVANIA	44
CALIFORNIA	49	MASSACHUSETTS	4	RHODE ISLAND	2
CANADA	4	MICHIGAN	80	SOUTH CAROLINA	10
COLORADO	3	MINNESOTA	2	TENNESSEE	39
CONNECTICUT	1	MISSISSIPPI	3	TEXAS	16
FLORIDA	13	MONTANA	3	UTAH	9
GEORGIA	22	NEBRASKA	1	VERMONT	1
IDAHO	3	NEVADA	3	VIRGINIA	16
ILLINOIS	12	NEW JERSEY	1	WASHINGTON	2
INDIANA	31	NEW MEXICO	6	WEST VIRGINIA	16
IOWA	1	NORTH CAROLINA	11	WISCONSIN	21
KANSAS	1	NORTH DAKOTA	5	WYOMING	1
Total 630				

BIG BOY UNITS				JANUARY 1976
ALABAMA	18	KENTUCKY	25	NORTH DAKOTA	4
ALASKA	2	LOUISIANA	7	OHIO	121
ARIZONA	13	MAINE		OKLAHOMA	5
ARKANSAS	6	MARYLAND	7	OREGON	
CALIFORNIA	107	MASSACHUSETTS	7	PENNSYLVANIA	59
CANADA	22	MICHIGAN	136	RHODE ISLAND	2
COLORADO	7	MINNESOTA	4	SOUTH CAROLINA	16
CONNECTICUT	3	MISSISSIPPI	7	SOUTH DAKOTA	4
DELAWARE		MISSOURI	5	TENNESSEE	59
FLORIDA	14	MONTANA	7	TEXAS	18
GEORGIA	30	NEBRASKA	5	UTAH	12
HAWAII	1	NEVADA	3	VERMONT	
IDAHO	7	NEW HAMPSHIRE		VIRGINIA	23
ILLINOIS	16	NEW JERSEY	5	WASHINGTON	5
INDIANA	30	NEW MEXICO	8	WEST VIRGINIA	19
IOWA	5	NEW YORK	3	WISCONSIN	33
KANSAS	4	NORTH CAROLINA	22	WYOMING	1
Total 917				

1968
President Marriott Restaurant Operations
Mike Hostage & wife Dorothy.

agement from his board, Bob began opening up relative to a merger, buy-out, etc. It wasn't a light Bob saw at the end of the tunnel, it was a train; and it was coming right at him. Boston's Waldorf organization was an early suitor, but Bob found they had little in common; but Hack Davenport of the J. R. Thompson Cafeteria operation in Chicago became a serious merger possibility. Bob, on the surface, became enthusiastic. I was not privileged to the merger talks, but my gut feeling was that Bob was looking for morality in a new association and

Judy & Bill Mariott, Fred Bell and Bob Wian

Bob Wian, Woody Marriott, Alex Schoenbaum and Bill Marriott

Bob Eakin, Manfred Bernhard, Harry Andrews and Bill Walker

Bob Wian, Bill Marriott, Gene Kilburg, Woody Marriott

their management rather than money. He did not want his company to be prostituted to the highest bidder. His entire success was built around relationships, and money always seemed to be secondary. He also had a massive ego to protect, particularly in relation to the employee franchise program and the pension trust fund, subjects on which Hack Davenport had mixed feelings.

Things didn't work out with the J. R. Thompson organization, and the next time we knew there was a new interest was when Woody Marriott arrived in Glendale and started meeting with our numbers people. Tall, lean, and taciturn, Woody Marriott was the opposite of what we were accustomed to from visiting firemen. Franchisees, suppliers, sales reps were people of impeccable manners and good will when in the presence of Bob or his associates, whether they be dish machine operators or board members. At the time, it was mentioned that Alex Schoenbaum, board member and then owner of Shoney's, based in Charleston,

From left: John & Esther Elias, Dottie & Len Dunagan, Lou Elias, Dee & Harry Matthews

From left: Margaret & Harley McDowell, John & Jane Doe, Eve & Larry Kunz, Dorothy & Ed Melton.

Bob & June Wian, Blanche & Jack Maier

Chris & Lola Hansen

West Virginia, had met with Woody Marriott and recommended a dialogue be opened with the possibility of tying the two companies together for the common good. Woody Marriott really shook us up. At first we were more amused by his charging around the premises, but it soon became apparent that the guy was serious. To some, Woody was cold and calculating, a big time numbers cruncher, and in learning more about the Marriott's, we got the feeling that Woody was not the shaker and mover, but more of an errand boy for brother Willard and others. Maybe he didn't have final authority to make the deal, but he sure had the clout to intimidate the always-trusting boys and girls at Bob's Home of the Big Boy.

Bob used power in the most constructive way possible; Marriott power in many cases was destructive. Bob built his constituency on power well utilized; Marriott built a corporation by using power that was at times deceptive and disruptive. In their defense, it's possible the Marriott Corporation hierarchy simply did not know any better. They were ill equipped to be good motivators regarding the management of restaurants and food service personnel in the Bob Wian style.

During a stroll outside the Old Post Office Building in Washington, D.C., at the time of the Nixon inauguration preparation, J. Willard Marriott told me that he attributed his success to having acquired choice locations for his restaurants and other real estate holdings early in his career. I thought it was a good measure of the man who would credit seemingly unrelated situations or events, which brought about monetary success. It should be noted it was wealth from Mrs. Marriotts family that provided principal funding that helped create the Marriott empire. Alice Marriott's stepfather was a U.S. Senator from Utah.

All of the Marriott hierarchy did have one thing in common with the Bob Wian Big Boy Family—beautiful, gracious, accomplished wives. In all my years around Bob's people, franchisees and suppliers, I never met one of their wives I didn't admire and respect. They were supportive to their husbands, and really the fellows couldn't have made it without them. Esther Elias, Judy Marriott, Betty Schoenbaum, Mary Kassab, Dorothy Hostage, Rosemary Elias, Donna Marriott, Helen Morgan, Lola Hansen, Becky Goehegan, Gloria Andrews, Jackie Boury, June Frejlach, Mickey Boury, Dottie Dunagan, Norma Azar, Kay Barringer, Gloria Ingham, and of course June Wian, to name just a few.

Major contributers to Big Boy's Fabulous '60s
Standing, from left: Virginia & Bob Glasset, Lola & Chris Hansen, Dee & Harry Matthews, Carl Thornton.
Seated, from left: Bob Eakin, Elmo & Becky Goehegan, Pat Eakin, and Dorothy Thornton.

The Official Publication of Big Boy Restaurants of America

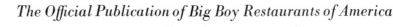

THE BIG BOY FAMILY NEWS

SUMMER 1968

Wian Leaves Presidency; Maintains Marriott Position

Bob Wian, Elmo Goehegan and Bob's son Chappie

Bob Wian, after 32 years of service to company and community, has announced his retirement as President of the Big Boy Restaurants of America.

Bob indicated his retirement is due to personal reasons and a wish for more taurants that he founded, is a suitable time to reiterate his uncompromising, unvaried philosophy of restaurant operation: The best quality food, at moderate prices, in spotless surroundings, served with courtesy and hospitality.

This philosophy has produced to date 23 Bob's Big Boy Family Restaurants in the greater Los Angeles area, and over 650 Big Boy Franchise restaurants, operating in 44 states, an eloquent and permanent testimonial.

BOB WIAN QUITS

What really happened to Bob Wian and his company is what is happening everywhere. People put their heart and soul into an enterprise, and it succeeds beyond their original vision. When that happens, as it did to Bob Wian, a brand new set of parameters sets in, at the cost of excellence. In Bob's case Big Boy was potentially too big for a board of directors to ignore. They wanted to expand at a minimum of two new units per year in southern California; Bob didn't. Some of Bob's best friends on the board also insisted that prices be increased. And to add insult to injury, they expected Bob to spend more time in the office. Later, when the deal closed with Marriott, everything hit the fan.

For example, J. Willard called Bob one morning at the office and, surprise surprise, no Bob. Bob was home; he wasn't about to do 9 to 5. He could run the company from his home, Lakeside Golf Club, or the Double Eagle, so he thought. Then when it was learned that his salary was more than J. Willard's, the Marriotts wanted to make a "slight" adjustment. And so it went. I resigned in the fall of 1967, effective when things on the table were completed, so I left on May 17, 1968—a six-month notice. Bob quit three days earlier but with no notice to anyone, cold turkey. That was certainly shocking in what turned out to be a controversial development!!

[BOB] "I tried to be inactive prior to the merger with Marriott, but in the restaurant business it is impossible to slow down. It's the tempo of the whole thing. The minute the conductor stops waving the baton, the whole thing just loses its pace, so I decided to quit. It happened on a Sunday in the backyard down on the dock at Toluca Lake. [I was] fishing with the kids, and I enjoyed it so much and realized how little time I had to do it, how little I was doing it. I was supposed to meet Bill Marriott the next day at the airport at 10:00. I picked him up, and by 2 o'clock I was walking out of my office with my briefcase, and I never went back."

Back row: June, Chappie, Bobby, Barbara.
Front: Julie, Bob, Casey

Back row: Bobby, Chappie,
Front: Barbara. Julie, Casey

What happened between 10:00 a.m. and 2:00 p.m. solidified Bob's decision to leave. Bill Marriott asked Bob to drive by a number of locations Bob thought might be good for additional Big Boy restaurants. After about 20 possibilities were looked at and discussed, Bob asked Bill which one or two he liked. Bill said he liked them all. Bob countered that resources would prohibit building more than a couple of new restaurants at a time. Bill said, "We've got all the money you need. Let's build them all." By resources, Bob meant money and superior personnel. To Bill Marriott, resources meant money. But Bill Marriott was not going to destroy the reputation of Bob's Big Boy food preparation and service, at least not with Bob Wian at the helm.

Quitting meant a new life, a family life. When you're home all the time in a wilderness area 55 miles from the San Fernando Valley, you really get to know your family, whether you like it or not. He liked it, because it gave him the opportunity to help develop their skills, which would open doors for them in the future. At the same time, it gave Bob and June an environmental serenity that fame and fortune many times cannot provide.

[BOB] "Now the reason I moved up to the ranch was [that] my social life at Lakeside would not enable me to spend the time I wanted with the kids. Up here we were doing something totally together in a completely different environment, which we have happily adjusted to, and, of course, it's a real good, wholesome endeavor."

Bob was not a happy camper after Marriott, but the ranch and family responsibilities gave him a time window to adjust to an endeavor that wouldn't particularly make the

Barbara

The Family

"Lifestyles of the Rich and Famous" show. Thank goodness. He had a great family.

Daughter Barbara worked for Bob as his secretary, followed by a retail clothing venture, before becoming an accomplished horsewoman, training and riding jumping horses in shows around the country. She later managed a riding school in Los Angeles. Barbara, who had attended Marymount College in Virginia, eventually returned to school at UCLA and received a degree as a drug and alcohol rehabilitation counselor. After an internship, she moved to Honolulu, where she practices her profession.

Son Chapman ("Chappie") did it all. After high school and a brief stay in college, followed by Air Force duty during, but not in, Vietnam, Chappie worked at Bob's Big Boy before moving to Valyermo to take over the Black Angus cattle operation. He won rodeo competitions, trained and broke horses on the ranch for others, including my daughter, who had an Arab filly. Movie star buddy, Kurt Russell and Chappie could and did dehorn, castrate, and brand calves with the best of them. He was also an expert swimmer, diver, and yachtsman. Diving from a 60-foot mainmast of Bob's schooner was child's play for Chap. He also had all the tools to be a professional baseball catcher, but not much with the bat. He had three approaches as a hitter: right, left, and once in a while. Chappie was also featured in the movie "Suds." Putting fun in the sun behind him, he opened Big Boy restaurants in Montreal, and later returned to Los Angeles as Director of Operations for the La Salsa Restaurant chain. Chappie now lives in Hawaii, where he owned and operated the Salsa Rita Restaurants for

Rancho Valyermo

many years. The restaurants have been sold, and Chappie, a full-time novelist, is finishing his fourth book. Chapman II, 28, is a professional photographer in Venice, California, and daughter Jenna lives at home.

Julie, the youngest, also spent time in the food service industry as a sales representative marketing health care products throughout Southern California. She now lives in Oregon. She has one son, Matthew.

Casey, named after Bob's great friend and fellow Valley National Bank board member Casey Stengel, is the West Coast Business News reporter for CNN. Casey was previously a writer-producer at Financial News Network, 1983-85. Later, he became a reporter covering aerospace and defense for Investors Daily, 1985-86; freelance reporting and marketing, 1987-88; and returned to CNN in 1988. In 1989, Casey was transferred to Washington, DC, as Bureau Chief. Casey, 40, graduated from the University of Southern California, where he was Editor of the Daily Trojan. Growing up at Valyermo, Casey received "hands on" knowledge of the cattle and fruit ranch business, while helping his dad and brother Chappie. Many thought Bob Wian was a low handicap golfer. No way. Casey was and is the golfer, who, with a little time for practice, would again be a scratch player.

Bob's wife, June, wrote me a letter in 1967, thanking me for something I had done for her children. That thoughtfulness on her part was typical of what this gracious and beautiful lady did for so many, particularly for her husband's female employees and associates. She

created the bridge club "Bidder Halves", fashion shows, "Better Halves" for wives of restaurant managers and was hostess at scores of the company's social affairs. June also created Bob's Seasoning Salt, appeared as spokeswoman in filmed television commercials for Bob's Salad Dressings and Sauces. That came easily for June, as she, at one time, had a successful career in the entertainment business with Earl Carroll Vanities and the famed Copacabana in New York. June was widowed in 1953 when her first husband, Fernand Baehler of New Orleans, Louisiana, died of a heart attack. June Wian was probably the best thing that ever happened to Bob, for in their 35 years of marriage, no one ever heard Bob express a discouraging word about June. Bob and June met in 1955 at Alphonse's Restaurant in Toluca Lake. It figures.

Yale University's Levi Noble, "the Papa of the San Andreas," spent his life living right on top of the famous fault, studying and mapping it. Where else, other than Dr. Noble's former ranch, would Bob Wian gamble and build the magnificent Rancho Valyermo (16,000 square feet under one roof)? Fit for a king on over 850 acres of lush and beautiful land devoted to 35,000 fruit trees on 40 acres, 100 acres of permanent pasture, 200 acres of alfalfa in full production, plus a big league cattle operation. The three million-dollar estate included five other houses of various sizes and age. Bob made more profit from the sale of Rancho Valyermo than from the sale of his company to Marriott. The Ranch sold for over 3.25 million, and the building cost of the home was only $350,000. The sale of Big Boy to Marriott was seven million, but only a modest portion of that went directly to Bob. Most of it went to the company's pension trust fund and increments of four to five percent to board members.

Rancho Valyermo is now in very good hands as a rest and relaxation facility for Los Angeles County firefighters. They never had it so good.

MARRIOTT QUITS BIG BOY

The company that Marriott acquired in 1967-68 was the most respected food service operation in the country. Marriott knew it, and that's why they went after the company they eventually let go. They really didn't want Big Boy, but they did want the power and prestige it would bring to the Marriott Corporation.

Many years before, Marriott had offered Bob Wian $25,000 for the franchise in Washington, D.C. They did not want to build Big Boy restaurants; they just didn't want any-

Marriott to Sell 104 Bob's Big Boys for $65 Million

By ANNE MICHAUD
SPECIAL TO THE TIMES

Come summer, 104 Boys will be looking for work.

Restaurant Enterprises Group Inc. of Irvine has agreed to buy 104 Bob's Big Boy restaurants in California from Marriott Corp. for $65 million. The family-style restaurants, famed for the signature statue of smiling boy holding a hamburger, will be converted to Coco's and Carrows.

The purchase, which also includes 16 Allie's restaurants in San Diego County, should be completed by early summer, said Mike Malanga, vice president of corporate development for Restaurant Enterprises.

As a result, the future of most of the chubby fiberglass Big Boys, which stand 4- to 8-feet-tall outside each restaurant, is uncertain. But some could be back before long.

"We will probably end up buying [the statues] and putting them in some of our new Big Boy restaurants around the country," said Tony Michaels, vice president marketing for Elias Bros. Restaurants Inc. of Detroit, which controls the franchise for more than 900 Big Boys in North America and Japan.

"We have a commitment for 10 to be built in the Los Angeles area in the next year or two, so some of those guys will be staying there," he said, noting that the company recently opened a Big Boy diner

in the Glendale Galleria, at the site of the original Bob's Big Boy.

Marriott sold the chain to Elias Bros. in 1987 but retained the right to use the Big Boy name. Marriott had bought the chain in 1967 from Bob Wian of Newport Beach, who opened the first Big Boy in Glendale in 1938. Wian modeled the Big Boy statue after a local 6-year-old who, according to legend, used to clean counters in exchange for Bob's double-decker burgers.

Besides Coco's and Carrows, Restaurant Enterprises Group runs El Torito, Reuben's, Charley Brown's, Baxter's and jojos restaurants. The company, the nation's 13th-largest food service firm, operates 514 restaurants with $900 million in sales in 1990, according to Nation's Restaurant News.

body else to build them. However, in 1963, Bob gave the franchise to his old friend, Bill Bemis, who eventually sold out to Marriott as previously mentioned.

It would be difficult to find another corporate giant like Marriott who could, in few short years, destroy a fabulously successful company like Bob's Big Boy. It's mind boggling, especially to thousands of employees and associates. Even the famous Los Angeles Dodgers Hot Dog was too much for the Marriott Corporation to prepare and serve at Dodger Stadium in Los Angeles.

The Bob's Big Boy on the original site in Glendale closed on Monday, October 16, 1989. On that date, the Los Angeles Times took a statement from Richard Sneld, a Marriott spokesman, to the effect that "the hotel and restaurant corporation has conducted surveys showing that 'people want a contemporary atmosphere and trendy food items at moderate prices.'"

When Bob Wian learned that the restaurant was going to be demolished for a mini-mall, he said, "I feel perfectly lousy about it."

Marriott, in other news releases, said that all of their remaining Bob's Big Boys would be converted to Allies, named for Alice Marriott, mother of the Marriott Chairman and President, J. W. Marriott, Jr.

They did try the concept in San Diego, and like most other restaurant operations they touched, it didn't work. Eventually, they sold the Big Boy operations to Restaurant Enterprises Group, Inc., of Irvine, California, who own Carrow's and Coco's. Many of Bob's Big Boys have been converted to Carrow's and Coco's. As reported in the Los Angeles Times in February 2001, Carrow's and Coco's filed for bankruptcy protection. FRD Acquisition Company filed the petition after deciding not to make a $9.8 million dollar payment on $167.6 million in debt securities. FRD's parent, Advantica Restaurant Group Inc. of South Carolina, put Coco's and Carrow's on the block last February to focus on Denny's restaurants, its core chain.

FOOTNOTES

Big Boy May Bow to Allie

Goodby, Bob; hello, Allie.

As part of Marriott Corp.'s plan to revamp some of its Bob's Big Boy coffee shops in California, two sons will show devotion to their mother.

The new name for the Big Boy units being remodeled in San Diego will be "Allie's Family Restaurant," or simply "Allie's." The name is in honor of Alice S. Marriott, mother of Marriott President and Chair-

Alice S. Marriott

man J. W. Marriott Jr. and his brother, Vice Chairman Richard E. Marriott.

If the experiment is successful, Marriott has said it may drop the chubby Big Boy and convert all 214 of its Bob's Big Boy diners. If the experiment is not successful, the Marriott boys may have some explaining to do.

Los Angeles Times
Vendor working for Marriott Corp. finds a hungry customer during game at Dodger Stadium.

A Dodger Dog?
Union Says Marriott Complained of Losses at Stadium

By THOMAS S. MULLIGAN
TIMES STAFF WRITER

Marriott Corp., which suffered through a nightmare rookie season last year running the food concessions at Dodger Stadium, may be off to a rough start in its sophomore year as well.

The union representing the stadium's 1,000 food workers says Marriott, complaining that it has lost money on the venture, is proposing "a whole host of take-aways" that could cut some workers' pay as much as 30%. Under the proposal, for example, vendors' commissions would drop to as low as 16% of sales from the 21.5% it has been since Dodger Stadium opened in 1962, union organizer Gary Guthman said.

Marriott's every move last year seemed to create controversy: doing away with grilled Dodger Dogs, forbidding a popular vendor from throwing bags of peanuts and ordering salespeople to keep working during the national anthem. It later reversed all three decisions.

Washington, D.C.-based Marriott and Local 11 of the Hotel Employees and Restaurant Employees Union are negotiating a contract to replace one that expires April 1. They have had one meeting, on Feb. 11, at which Marriott outlined its proposal. The next meeting is Wednesday.

Robert T. Souers, a Marriott vice president for corporate information, said the union is not portraying Marriott's proposal accurately, but he declined to be specific. He said he expects an amicable settlement before the April 1 deadline.

Souers also declined to say how much money Marriott lost at Dodger Stadium last year, but he said: "To rectify the situation, we're looking to both increase sales and reduce costs in the year ahead."

Union sources said Marriott managers told them that the losses were substantial.

If Marriott could lose money last year—when the
Please see STADIUM, D3

STADIUM: Union Tells of Marriott Loss

Continued from D1

Dodgers led the National League with attendance of 3.3 million—it was either because of bad management or because it made a "low-ball" bid to wrest the contract away from the vendor who had held it 29 years, Guthman said Thursday.

An executive of the Florida company that helped Marriott develop its Dodger Stadium bid said the deal should be a money-maker.

"If it had been supervised and managed properly, it could have turned a profit," said Kenneth J. Young, executive vice president of New Vista Services Inc. of Tampa.

New Vista is suing Marriott for $10.75 million for allegedly breaching a partnership agreement under which the firms bid successfully on food-service contracts for Dodger Stadium; the Salt Palace in Salt Lake City, home of the Utah Jazz basketball team, and Reunion Arena in Dallas, home of the Dallas Mavericks.

New Vista charges that Marriott used New Vista's expertise and reputation in the arena concessions business to help it win the contracts, then dumped New Vista in December, 1990, once the bids were accepted.

Marriott does not comment on matters in litigation, Souers said.

Marriott got into trouble recently when the real estate slump made it impossible to unload hotels and nursing homes it built with the intention of selling, according to analyst Michael G. Mueller of Montgomery Securities in San Francisco.

As a result, it now carries $3.6 billion in debt, interest on which is dragging earnings down.

Mueller said Marriott's strategy is to build up its service businesses, such as stadium concessions and hotel management, but decrease its capital-intensiveness—that is, get less involved in developing or owning hotels and other real estate.

Shark Bait!

BOB WIAN'S FUNERAL

And now the end is near,
And so I face the final curtain.
My friend, I'll say it clear,
I'll state my case,
Of which I'm certain.
I've lived a life that's full,
I traveled each and every highway.
And more, much more than this,
I did it My Way.

Paul Anka

IN LOVING MEMORY OF

ROBERT CHARLES WIAN

ENTERED THIS LIFE
JUNE 15, 1914
PENNSYLVANIA

ENTERED ETERNAL LIFE
MARCH 31, 1992
NEWPORT BEACH, CALIFORNIA

FUNERAL SERVICE
THURSDAY APRIL 2, 1992
11:00 am
PACIFIC VIEW MEMORIAL CHAPEL
NEWPORT BEACH, CALIFORNIA

OFFICIANT
FATHER JOHN STONER

INTERMENT
PRIVATE

DIRECTORS
PACIFIC VIEW MORTUARY

On March 9, 1992, Bob suffered a cerebral hemorrhage and was found unconscious by his wife June in their Newport Beach home. Earlier in the day, Bob was in a minor one-car accident in which he apparently lost his equilibrium while he was driving. Doctors believe his brain began hemorrhaging earlier in the day. Robert Charles Wian died on March 31, 1992. He was 77.

His accident was well publicized in all media, including the Los Angeles Times, Daily News, Associated Press, Orange County News, the Newport Beach News Pilot, television and radio. However, his death was not widely known until the day before the funeral. Nevertheless, the Pacific View Memorial Chapel was filled, with standing room only inside and out. It was a short, simple ceremony, in keeping with Bob's wishes. It was officiated by Father John Stoner. While Bob was not a Catholic, wife June is, and they were both active supporters of the Priory adjoining their former ranch in Valyermo, California. All of the children were there, Chappie, Barbara, Casey, Julie. Also attending were Len Dunagan and wife

Robert Wian, founder of Bob's Big Boy, in serious condition with cerebral hemorrhage

By Iris Yokoi
Staff Writer

NEWPORT BEACH — Bob's Big Boy restaurant founder and former Glendale mayor Robert C. Wian remained in serious condition at Hoag Hospital Thursday after suffering a cerebral hemorrhage earlier this week.

Wian, 77, was admitted to the hospital's intensive care unit Monday night, after his wife June found him uncon-scious in their Big Canyon home, according to son Casey.

Earlier in the day, Wian was in a minor car accident, in which he apparently lost his equilibrium while driving and struck a tree in the Fashion Island area, but doctors believe his brain began hemorrhaging before he even got into his car, Casey said.

Wian has suffered some paralysis and is being treated with medication, but it's still too early to tell whether any brain damage has occurred, according to his son. "He's stabilized and improving," Casey said Thursday.

Wian built his restaurant empire from the ground up. Selling his car for $250 and borrowing another $50 from his father, Wian opened the original Bob's restaurant in Glendale in 1936 as a 10-seat hamburger stand called Bob's Pantry.

The name was later changed to the well-known Bob's Big Boy, after one of his regular customers — a suspender-clad boy who routinely ordered a double-decker cheeseburger.

In 1967, Wian sold the restaurant chain to the Marriott Corp., which began converting many of the restaurants into Allie's coffee shops. Last year, Marriott sold its 120 Bob's and Allie's to Irvine-based Restaurant Enterprises Group, which plans to turn them into Coco's and Carrow's restaurants in coming years, leaving only 16 privately fran-chised Bob's Big Boy restaurants in Cali-fornia.

Wian also became one of Glendale's youngest City Council members when he was elected to the council in 1948 at age 34. He later served as mayor.

Even after selling to Marriott, Wian
See WIAN/Back Page

Dottie, Tom Holman and wife Pat, Rudy Martinez and wife Netta, Barney Dale and wife Dorothy, Dr. George Towne and wife Sally. Former managers, friends, neighbors, Manfred Bernhard and of course, Lou Elias and Bill Morgan from Michigan.

The gathering was not particularly solemn as old friends got together, and because June Wian knew Bob best, the service was quick, the food was delicious, and the atmosphere upbeat and casual.

Many of the old Big Boy family had made room for people they didn't really know, friends who came into Bob and June's lives after Big Boy. As would be expected, we made sure the customers were taken care of, and most of us stood at the rear of the chapel. Only when the organist began to play "My Way" did things get a little heavy. Tears began to fall, composure became difficult, but the old guard made sure the customers were not unduly disturbed. After all, one doesn't lose control when there are guests to be considered. Bob Wian would have it no other way. Why change now? Even though "My Way" was appropriate and sad, those who knew Bob best could rejoice that they worked for and with an original. There would never be another. Just ask the people that knew him.

Over a year later, on July 23, 1993, Bob's youngest son Casey wrote:

"Bob Wian was the greatest man I've ever, or will ever, know.

Sure, I'm biased—he was my Dad. But virtually everyone whose life he touched came away richer for it. His employees and business associates profited financially. His friends were enriched by his zest for life and his generosity. Our family had everything anyone could ever want—most importantly, his love.e.

"After Dad passed away, several newspaper reporters called to ask what kind of man he was. I struggled for the right words. A year later, I think I've come up with a better answer: he was a paradox.

"Bob was a daring entrepreneur who revolutionized the restaurant business, yet his clothes were 20 years out of date. He once went

to a Mercedes dealership and paid cash—one for Mom, one for him—but he was constantly yelling at us to turn off the lights! 'You're killing me with the electricity bill!' [He would say]. We swore Norman Lear modeled Archie Bunker after Dad, but when in a time of racial intolerance I angered his all-white country club friends by naively showing up to play golf with my black principal, he stuck up for me.e.

"Today we often hear people espousing traditional family values, criticizing anti-establishment types who only live for the moment. Dad was a perfect mixture of the best of both worlds. Of course, I'll never forget Dad. But neither will the thousands of others who knew Bob."

LET'S HEAR IT
FOR THE ELIAS BROTHERS

Bob Wian wrote the following a newspaper column in the summer of 1969.

"Fred, Lou and John Elias, three guys who started on a shoestring and built a business and a circle of friends and admirers which is seldom equaled. Three guys who embody individually and collectively philosophies that are nice. Three guys who are good to be with; who are a pleasure to talk about; and enrich one's outlook on life by just being in their company. They seem to have, as is many times the case, also surrounded themselves with others in their business who embody and reflect these same qualities.

In my thirty-some-odd-years with Big Boy I have made many dear friends and from each one I have endeavored to exemplify the qualities they have. The three boys in Detroit, whom I am proud to say

Big Boy Franchiser Files for Chapter 11

■ **Restaurants:** Owner Elias Bros. will sell company to an investor. Chain has had problems with growth, cash flow.

From Associated Press

DETROIT—The franchiser of the Big Boy restaurant chain has filed for Chapter 11 bankruptcy protection, the company said Friday.

Elias Bros. Corp. also said it will sell the company to investor Robert G. Liggett Jr.

The Warren, Mich.-based chain includes 455 Big Boy eateries.

The purchase price was not disclosed but will be made public next week, said Anthony Michaels, Elias' chief executive. The sale is subject to approval by the U.S. Bankruptcy Court.

Michaels said the agreement should end speculation about the future of the chain, which has had difficulties with recent expansions as well as cash-flow problems.

"The stores are open, the Big Boy icon goes on," Michaels said. "That line in 'Austin Powers'— 'He's always been around'—well, that still holds true."

The Big Boy statue, which is prominently displayed outside Big Boy restaurants, was featured in both "Austin Powers" movies as

the vehicle in which Austin Powers' nemesis Dr. Evil escaped into outer space.

The company was founded by Fred, Louis and John Elias, who ran small restaurants in the Detroit area after World War II. They later offered to franchise the family-style restaurant to Bob Wian, who founded Bob's Big Boy in California.

Big Boy purchased 34 Shoney's restaurants in October 1998 to expand its national presence. But the conversion took longer than expected. Elias Bros. fell behind with creditors and had to renegotiate vendor contracts last fall.

The company last month closed 43 Big Boy restaurants in Pennsyl-

vania, West Virginia, Ohio and Michigan. But Michaels said business remained good at the remaining restaurants.

Elias Bros. had several offers on the table and reached a purchase agreement with one investment group in August. But that deal fell through and Liggett stepped in, Michaels said.

"Mr. Liggett is very committed to this sales process," Michaels said. "We want everyone to understand that Big Boy restaurants worldwide will be fully operational during the reorganization."

Liggett is the founder and chairman of Liggett Broadcast Group, which merged this year with **Citadel Communications** Co.

[The reporter innocently insinuated Big Boy started in Detroit. It originated in Glendale, CA. in 1937]

are among my dearest friends, though they differ in appearance and may differ in their personalities and differ to some degree in their tastes, think as one on those certain things that give a meaning to life.

This is the Elias brothers; and is a tribute to their father, recently departed, to whom much of the credit for the nice things they have done rightfully belongs."

Years ago the late John Elias sent me a couple of anecdotes regarding his and his brother's great relationship with Bob Wian.

"One night Bob and I had been out drinking. I guess on this

one particular night we just had one or two too many. We arrived back in our hotel room in the wee hours of the morning. We went right to sleep. I woke up hours later to go to the bathroom and saw him sitting up in bed drinking buttermilk. I said, "Bob, what the hell are you doing up at 6:30 a.m. We just went to bed." He looked at his watch through his pink eyes and said, "I'll be damned, I've got my watch on upside down. I thought it was 12:00."

In another humorous incident: For years my brothers and I entertained Bob a great deal. Bob entertained us a great deal. Bob went to bed exhausted quite often. Then, after several years of this good fellowship, Bob looked at two of us who were with him late that night and excitedly exclaimed. "Well I'll be damned. I've finally got it all figured out why you guys are always so fresh and I'm always so pooped. I just realized it. Most of the time there is just two of you. One is always resting."

My brothers and I can never forget Bob for the great influence he has had on our lives. We will always be grateful to him."

Big Boy International Franchisee

Michigan Big Boy Fan Club!

WHAT ABOUT BOB?

BIG BOY BIG BOY
KING OF THEM ALL

BIG BOY BIG BOY
HAD A BIG FALL

ALL THE FINE WOMEN
AND ALL THE GOOD MEN

COULDN'T PUT BIG BOY BACK TOGETHER AGAIN

UNTIL NOW !

Seven years before Robert G."Bob" Liggett was born Robert C."Bob" Wian created the original double deck hamburger the Big Boy. Now 65 years later a new era for Big Boy is taking shape due to the purchase by Liggett of the Big Boy name, Elias Bros. Big boy restaurants, FLJ food technology and Main Event Catering. The new name is Big Boy Restaurants International. Liggett bought the famous symbol after financial difficulties created by the previous management. Bob Liggett's goal, in my opinion, is to bring Big Boy back as the nations most famous food service symbol and with a name like "Bob" this long time Big Boy customer will make it work because he knows how to do things successfully.

Another plus; the entire Liggett family has long supported Big Boy. Mrs. Liggett 'Vicki' was a Big Boy waitress while attending high school and during the summers while a student at Michigan State. Bob's brother, John was a bus boy and then a cook by the time he was eighteen. Liggett children, Emily and twins Roberta and Marjorie as well as Bob's, mother, Ellen, will lend support to this ambitious enterprise.

Bob Liggett is no stranger to success. His expertise in the broadcast industry as owner operator of radio stations across the country is well known. Starting at age 14 as a gofer at WPON in Pontiac Michigan, Bob was encouraged by his father, a writer, actor, and U.S. Army communications expert. Mention Bob Sr. to those in the business and one immediately thinks of the Lone Ranger, the Green Hornet, Sgt. Preston and scores of radios super stars; Gene Autry, Roy Rogers, Sky King, and a host of comedy and mystery programs of that golden age.

Bob Jr. learned from the best but better than that knew what to do with opportunity. Simply put, the acquisition of FM radio stations, one at a time, until the still young man became one the countries most successful in broadcasting.

After spending time with Bob, here in California, I saw some of the same characteristics that Bob Wian practiced on a daily basis. No flim flam, no bull, just a wholesome positive attitude toward the customer, the employee and Big Boy reputation, the most well know image in the food service industry.

In the fall of 2000, Elias Brother's with a debt of $100 million went bankrupt due to over-expansion outside of their Michigan base where they continue to do very well. Bob Liggett, owner/operator of radio stations is now the owner of the Big Boy trade mark. He assumed approximately twenty-five percent of the debt of the Elias Brother corporation. The new corporation is called Big Boy Restaurants International, which includes Elias Brother's Corp., Big Boy Restaurant and Market, FLJ Food Technology and Manufacturing Co. and Main Event Catering.

With a name like Bob, Liggett just might bring back the glory days of Big Boy.

Big Boy Takes Pepsi Challenge, Drops Coke as Chain's Cola

From Associated Press

DETROIT—After 65 years with Coca-Cola, Big Boy Restaurants announced it's switching to Pepsi.

The restaurant chain known for its boy mascot with a round belly and black pompadour hairstyle said Monday that all of its 170 hamburger outlets would switch to Pepsi, immediately.

"It wasn't easy. Sixty-five years is a long time," said Tony Michaels, chief executive of Big Boy Restaurants. "But the package Pepsi put together allowed us to make the decision. Ultimately, they ended up winning the business because of a great, interesting proposal."

Terms of the deal were not disclosed.

Though Big Boy is small in the world of American franchise restaurants, "Every drop counts" in the bitter battle between the world's soda mammoths, said John Sicher, editor of Beverage Digest

magazine in Bedford Hills, N.Y.

"It's a good win for Pepsi, but not a devastating defeat for Coke," Sicher said. "Conversely, in the cola wars, every drop that one sells, the other doesn't. They battle everywhere for every case."

Coke is the "800-pound gorilla" of soda fountain sales, with about 60% of the market, Sicher said. In recent years, Pepsi has been aggressively fighting to get a bigger piece of the pie.

Coca-Cola Co. spokesman Scott Williamson said it is common for companies to switch between the soft drink giants.

The agreement guarantees **Pepsi-Cola** Co. and Lipton exclusivity for fountain beverages, frozen carbonated beverages and bottles-to-go for the next five years.

Warren, Mich.-based **Big Boy Restaurants International** is the exclusive worldwide franchiser of Big Boy Restaurants in the United States, Japan and Egypt.

Robert G. "Bob" Liggett

BIG BOY WILL LIVE FOREVER

Pasadena Tournament of Roses January 1, 2002

Bob Eubanks and Stephanie Edwards parade co-hosts for many years sound off about Bob's Big Boy on KTLA Channel 5, now owned by the Chicago Tribune.

"Oh boy, here's one of my favorite floats. I went to Glendale High School for a few years, then to Pasadena High School. I used to hang out at Bob's Big Boy all the time. Taking a look at the good times of 1950's style the City of Glendale salutes a great American Institution of the Drive In Restaurant with Rock Around The Clock. Glendale was the first location for Bob's Big Boy in 1936. In fact I went to high-school with Bob Wian's son Bobby."

Stephanie, a Southern California favorite for many years remarked with humor,

> "I thought you were the model for the Big Boy. You kind of resemble him". One could put the multi talented Eubanks in Big Boy's back pocket. (It should be noted that Bob's Big Boy carhops never used rollerskates.)

On November 7, 1992, the California Historical Resources Commission voted seven to one to support the designation of the Bob's Big Boy Restaurant in the Toluca Lake section of Burbank and North Hollywood as a State Historical Landmark. The restaurant now becomes one of 54 in Los Angeles County. Built in 1949 and opened in 1950, it became the sixth original Bob's designed by Architect Wayne McAllister. (McAllister also designed the Sands Hotel in Las Vegas as well as the first hotel on the strip, the El Rancho Vegas.) Famed football player Frankie Albert was one of the owners. The other five have been torn down, including the original Bob's in Glendale in 1990.

It is interesting to note that the land owner of the site on which the new historical landmark sits is Philip R. MacDonald of Newport Beach, whose father built it for his longtime friend, Big Boy founder, Robert C. Wian. Scott MacDonald was one of Bob's most loyal associates and supporters, as well as a board member for many, many years. Ironically, in a battle that lasted more than a year, Philip MacDonald initially fought the designation. Journalist Wendy Wadnick of the Glendale New Press put it this way: "In an ironic twist of fate, the man who wanted to tear down a popular local eatery was instead honored for returning it to it's original glory." Phil's dad would be proud that his son lost the battle but won the war.

Furthermore, the restaurant is probably the most successful coffee shop in the country doing gross sales of over 4.876 million dollars in 2001 with none of the sales coming from alcoholic beverages. The restaurant operation is owned by a former Marriott staffer, Steve Funkhouser. Steve lives in Virginia, but long-time Big Boy manager Mark McCabe operates the restaurant.

The true key to Big Boy's future success would be to return to Big Boy's original formula and presentation. For 34 years the Big Boy hamburger was served with a half-tissue wrap and placed in an illustrated, four-color glassine bag. It was "The Original Meal on a Bun," "Twice as Big, Twice as Good." It was special. It did take a little extra effort and skill to properly half-wrap the Big Boy in a folded tissue and then place it in a bag, and it did cost a little more. Discontinuing that practice is what killed the totally unique presentation that Bob Wian created.

The only way the Big Boy hamburger will ever again take its place as the great sandwich it is to grill the three pieces of the sesame seed bun, the center on both sides, and place "The King of Them All" in a heat-retention wrap and bag, totally different from all the imitators. If it was good enough to be the best for 34 years, it is good enough now.

The most successful hamburger operation in southern California is the aforementioned In 'N Out, with 140 stores and growing. They half-wrap their hamburger in tissue, and then place the warm sandwich in a full-color, illustrated glassine bag. If Big Boy operators did the same, they would experience once again the popularity of the Original Big Boy Hamburger. That is, of course, if the original recipe and preparation are restored.

Battle for a Bob's Big Boy
Newport Man Hopes to Raze Place; Others Fight for It

By SUSAN CHRISTIAN
TIMES STAFF WRITER

P hilip MacDonald has a lifelong history with the Bob's Big Boy in Burbank.

His dad built the neon-lit coffee shop in 1949, when MacDonald was a year old. In the early '60s, he and his high school buddies hung out there slurping "the world's thickest malts" and munching "famous double-deck hamburgers." His teen-age sister, Lynn, waited tables at the Bob's.

Yet despite all the warm memories, MacDonald harbors little nostalgia for his old haunt—so little that he wants to level the place. Nostalgia, he complains, is what has gotten him and his family into a fix.

For the past six months, the Newport Beach developer has been battling Los Angeles preservationists over a most unlikely subject: this funky, throwback-to-the-'50s cafe on the busy intersection of Riverside Drive and Alameda Avenue near NBC studios.

Determined preservationists consider the coffee shop a local treasure that epitomizes the architectural style of its era. MacDonald views it as only a . . . well, a Bob's.

Last month, the Los Angeles County Board of Supervisors sided with the preservationists—voting to nominate the eatery as a state Historic Point of Interest. The California Office of Historic Preservation will consider the Bob's in Burbank for that title of distinction at a hearing in November.

MacDonald, 44, his recently widowed mother and three siblings are concerned about preserving something else: their option to convert the site into another use.

"You can't deal with [nostalgia] rationally," MacDonald said. "I have fondness for a lot of buildings, too, but that doesn't mean their owners' freedom of choice should be taken away."

The restaurant has been in MacDonald's family since his father, a Glendale home builder, erected it 43 years ago as a favor of sorts for longtime pal Robert C. Wian.

In 1936, Wian established the first Bob's restaurant in Glendale and, running short on cash a few restaurants later, persuaded Scott MacDonald to foot the bill for the sixth Big Boy eatery. The restaurateur leased the coffee shop and the land

Please see BOB'S, D7

Fred Bell, Bob Wian, Frankie Albert &
mother Albert, Scott McDonald and
Arnold Petersen.

Bob's gets historic recognition

By Paul R. Hubler
City Editor

A state panel in Sacramento gave final approval Friday to a proposal to make the Bob's Big Boy eatery in Toluca Lake a "California Point of Historical Interest."

The state Historical Resources Commission voted 7-1 to support the designation after a hearing, bringing to a halt a months-long feud between preservationists and a property owner who wanted to ...urant to erect

...id the Bob's ...rside Drive, ...dest remain- ...ation and is ...ombines the ...derne coffee ...the drive-in ...e emerging

[plaque:]
Big Boy
THIS RESTAURANT WAS BUILT IN 1949 BY
LOCALS SCOTT MacDONALD AND WARD ALBERT
AND IS THE OLDEST REMAINING BOB'S FAMILY
RESTAURANT IN AMERICA. IT WAS DESIGNED
BY RESPECTED ARCHITECT WAYNE McALLISTER
INCORPORATING THE 1940s TRANSITIONAL
DESIGN OF STREAMLINE MODERN STYLE WHILE
ANTICIPATING THE FREEFORM 50s COFFEE SHOP
ARCHITECTURE. THE TOWERING BOB'S SIGN IS
AN INTEGRAL PART OF THE BUILDING'S DESIGN
AND ITS MOST PROMINENT FEATURE.

STATE OF CALIFORNIA
POINT OF HISTORICAL INTEREST

Acton, California $2,500...firm   A Cincinatti Original...priceless

MEMORABILIA AND COLLECTORS

A Big Boy bobblehead doll sells for $500. A ceramic Big Boy, $300. Ceramic Big Boy ashtrays, salt and peppers, are $250. An original Big Boy menu, circa 1938, is priceless. A store in Las Vegas, Nevada, Antiquities, had a four-foot Big Boy statue for sale at $7,500.00.

In 1965, Joe Troiano, former owner of Lord Menu Co., printed a replica of the original, and even that imitation has great value. To differentiate between the two, look for the Lord Menu logo on the back of the imitation menu and Copyright 1938 on the original.

After 1968, plastic and lesser quality Big Boy collectibles were produced. Prior to 1968, the jewelry, Big Boy key-chains, money clips, cufflinks, and tie-tacks, were of very high quality. Figurines were always ceramic and the prices always fair. A bobblehead Big Boy doll sold for $5.00. Jewelry was sold at cost or given away. Even a solid gold three-dimensional Big Boy, which was given to a select group of Big Boy old-timers, was until lately not sold or traded. Bob Wian never authorized the manufacture of collectibles for their profit potential. To the contrary, his motivation was the advertising and public relations value these gifts provided.

Steve Soelberg has the finest collection of Big Boy memorabilia. While not a "dealer", as others are, Steve nevertheless is still looking for quality Big Boy artifacts to add to his collection. Sellers can contact Steve by calling 818-889-9909.

An odd coincidence? Four of the most knowledgable Big Boy aficianados in the USA live within ten miles of each other but rarely communicate. -C. Hansen

Small portion of Soleberg collection

A TRIBUTE

Putting this book project together brings back memories, some good, some bad. That should be expected. Bob Wian was my boss, and all in his family are still very dear to me, but I've tried to not make a "puff piece" out of this story. However, some things are very important to me personally, and they give reasons why much on these pages is flattering to Bob.

I had and have a speech impediment that I can disguise quite well when necessary. In 1955, I was finishing my B.A. requirements on the G.I. Bill and asked Hal Avery, a professor of marketing, what I might do in the advertising field. He had observed me quite closely over a two-year period and should have been expert in his advice. Professor Avery recommended I concentrate on employment that did not require public speaking or speaking in general. Specifically, he said, look for a company which needs a house organ to put out every month or so." This was just the opposite of what I wanted to do - to be an account executive at an ad agency.

At the same time, Bill Michaeljohn of Paramount Pictures told my wife, who was a contract player at Paramount in years past, to tell me to get the office boy job at a large advertising agency. It was good advice but hard to execute.

Finally, I got the office boy job at Hixon & Jorgensen Advertising Agency. For nine months, I waited on the executives and clients and was eventually promoted to the Traffic Department. During my months as an office boy (I was 28 years old with a wife and son), I got to know all the brass and frequently asked them if they would give me an assignment I could work on my own time.

Because I rode to and from work with one of the art directors, Frank Hubbard, any ideas I had could be put down in layout form for the appropriate account executive. Frank would submit my concepts, along with others he had gotten from the copywriters and account executive. No one at the client level really knew or cared where the ideas came from. To make a long story short, I created headlines and layouts for full-page ads in Time, Life, and Newsweek while making $200 a month as an office boy. Nobody knew but Frank and me. I really thought I had some talent and a good chance to be an account executive, and when an opening did arise for a junior account executive, I was sure I had a shot at it. Rather, I got shot at when Senior Vice President Tyler McDonald told me my speech problem would prohibit me from ever reaching my goal at Hixon & Jorgensen.

I had worked on food accounts for the agency, covering live TV shows—Time for Beany (Stan Freeberg, Walker Edmiston, and Daws Butler were the voice-over talent doing these daily live programs. Ed Reimer's "You're in good hands with Allstate" was the announcer), Sheriff John—with copy, product, props, displays, etc. I therefore began looking for a job in the food field, away from the politics of a big time advertising agency. Understand this wasn't a normal job search where qualifications are appearance, character, and other good things. This was a crusade to get a job where advancement was built on ability, of which I thought I had plenty..

A few weeks later, I was sitting in the Helen Edwards Agency on Wilshire Boulevard in Los Angeles, at the time the best of the advertising profession placement firms. It was lunchtime, and Helen was filling in at the reception desk when the phone rang. While Helen talked and took notes from someone looking for an advertising manager for a food concern, I couldn't help but assume I might have a chance. She was always available to talk to me, so I asked if she would put me on the list she was going to submit. She didn't refer to my speech problem, but said I wasn't as qualified as the client would like. Taking another angle, I asked in what part of Los Angeles the company was located. I explained that I had hoped to buy a house on the G.I. Bill and wondered if nobody on her list was hired, I would become a candidate. She wouldn't tell me, but I noticed when she was taking notes that the telephone prefix was OR. That's really all I needed to know.

I went back to the office, found out where the OR was located, then called the Chamber of Commerce in Inglewood and asked them the names of the major food companies. Bingo. Two weeks later, I met with John McCarty, Vice President of the Frito Company, Dallas, Texas, fully-controlled the speech problem and got the job. $500 a month, company car, beautiful office, great secretary, the best snack food company in the world. What more could a guy ask? It was later, even after I had done an outstanding job for Frito, that Booz Allen Hamilton, John McCarty and others were instrumental in my not getting a shot at a promotion with more responsibility, money and prestige, because, as John McCarty said later "You should have told me about your stutter." I said, "John, I wouldn't have gotten the job."

When I resigned in January of 1959 to look elsewhere, C. E. Doolin, then CEO and creator of Fritos in his mother's kitchen in San Antonio in 1932, offered me a vice presidency at double my salary to come to Dallas and work with him on new product ideas and possibly a restaurant concept he had always wanted to explore. He knew my Big Boy background, but he knew more about food service and food preparation than I did. C. E. Doolin was the finest human being I have ever known. We became acquainted more at Disneyland than elsewhere because Fritos had a concession in Frontierland and Doolin was developing a Ta-Cup corn masa creation and Jalapeno Bean Dip.

I had written and produced a documentary called "Adventures In Disneyland" which was very successful, and Doolin seemed appreciative that I had made it for him rather than the company. Later I would see him at a resort in Chandler, Arizona where he would hide out with his family from the corporate world that in my view he did not enjoy. We had a great rapport that no one knew anything about over my four-year association with the company. He could talk to me, knowing I was not politically motivated for selfish purposes.

Back to Bob Wian. When the Marriott's and all their troops came to the Century Plaza Hotel in Los Angeles for what was to be the formality of joining forces with the Big Boy franchisees, a series of business meetings took place. Beautifully printed programs, high-powered guest speakers, special entertainment, fashion shows, pre-planned lunch/dinner menus, plus, of course, the formal dinner dance with the "society band."

On the first morning of the first day, Bob Wian was to give the welcoming speech to bring everyone together for the common good. Now understand, this was a big deal. On one side, a bunch of entrepreneurs who, for the most part, earned every dollar they had with hard work, a lot of guts, and a particular faith in what Bob Wian had given them in the form of guidance and inspiration. On the other side, the Marriott group, trying to not interfere, bringing to the table good will, a helping hand, and expertise in areas that may be helpful to the Big Boy family. There was a problem, however; Bob Wian was not comfortable with the Marriott's. The meeting was to start at 9:00 a.m. sharp with Bob's welcome and opening speech.

The meeting was to start at 9 AM sharp, however at 8:55, Bob got up from his seat at the head table, came over to me, bent down and quietly said, "Take over." Years later, when I asked Bob how he could place so much responsibility at such a critical time, especially with the speech problem I had, he said, "Well the thing I saw most was the courage that it took to do it, not looking at the impediment. That's like a guy entering a race with one leg; I mean you've got to give a guy a lot of credit for doing it, and then eventually with enough courage it's going to be overcome. The guy that I really don't have respect for is the one that is doing half as much as he is capable of. The one I really respect is the one that does twice as much as he's capable of doing. He's the real thing."

Some of us spend our entire lives trying to prove that we are not failures. Bob Wian spent his proving that anyone can be successful if given the opportunity.

I never saw Bob Wian pout in front of others, never heard him belittle anybody with more than two people in the room including himself, never heard him preach, but always saw in Bob a willingness to help others realize their goals. He was a winner, and he let a lot of us tag along. Thanks for the ride, Bob. It was a great trip.

To Whom It May Concern:

In 1970 Bob Wian said the Big Boy story should be told and I was the one who should tell it.

Mr Wian...it was a pleasure. Lots of pictures.   C.H.

P.S. Why it took so long is something else. It's called "Bring 'em Young", J. Willard Marriott's (Sr) Mormon Mafiesque, an amusing short story about the long arm of corporate power, greed, and arrogance. Things I've kept in the closet for 35 years. Available late fall 2002.

There Was Business . . .

There Was Sociability

More from the Archives - Too Good To Leave Out

THE ORIGINAL
BIG-BOY HAMBURGER .15

(Served on a Toasted Bun with Our Special
Relish, Mayonnaise, Lettuce and Cheese.)

WE CUT OUR OWN
SPECIAL STEAK .35

(Choice 6 oz. Spencer Cut. Grilled to Your
Likeness and Served with Toasted Bun,
Potatoes, and Relish.)

KANSAS CITY
STEAK SANDWICH .25

(Tender Cut of Choice Beef. Grilled in Butter
and Served on Toasted Bread with Lettuce,
Tomato and Mayonnaise.)

SPAGHETTI & CHILI .25

(Generous Portion of Spaghetti with Chili and
Cheese Served with a Toasted Bun.)

SIZE .25

(Ground Steak with Chili and Beans or Spaghetti and Chili. Served with Toasted Bun
and Plenty of Fresh Chopped Onions.)

T-BONE STEAK .50

(A Tender 10-oz. T-Bone Cut. Served with
Hashed Browned Potatoes, Toasted Bun and
Our Own Relish.)

GROUND ROUND-TIP STEAK .35

(Choice Ground Beef Tastily Grilled with Potatoes, Bun, and Relish.)

TOASTED SANDWICHES

Lettuce and Tomato	.15
Toasted Cheese	.15
(Grilled in Butter)	
Fresh Tuna	.15
Bacon and Cheese	.20
Bacon and Tomato	.20
Bacon and Egg	.25
Ham and Egg	.25

THIN PANCAKES

(Grilled to a Golden Brown. Served with Melted Butter and Piping Hot
Maple Syrup.)

3 Pancakes, plain	.10
3 Pancakes with Ham, Bacon or 2 Fried Eggs	.25

THICK MALT (Our Special) .15
(So Thick You Eat It With a Spoon.)

Major Coffee (enjoy a second cup on us)	.05
Talbots Milk or Buttermilk	.05
Hires Root Beer	.05
Hires Rootbeer Float	.10
Nestles Hot Chocolate (With Pure Whipped Cream)	.10
Coca Cola	.05
Delaware Punch	.05
7-Up	.05

CHILI DISHES

Chili and Beans	.15
Chili Straight	.20
Tamale and Chili	.25
Spaghetti and Chili	.25
Choice of Fresh Pies for Dessert	.10

WE GRIND OUR OWN HAMBURGER AND MAKE OUR OWN CHILI FROM FINEST INGREDIENTS

Gene Autry sidekick Pat Buttram amuses with Mormon critique - Bill & Donna Marriott, particularly.

A Big Boy Family get-together - Deauville, Miami, Florida 1962

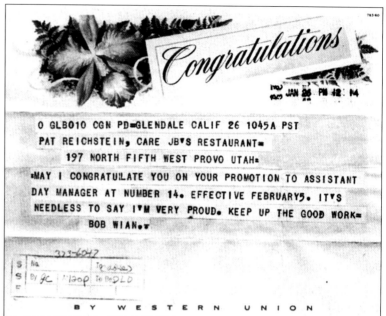

Pat Reichstein, now 64, advanced 25% of the printing cost of the Bob's Big Boy Story

Sportscaster Chick Hearn...style and class, the best in the business.

"The Front Yard"
9956 Toluca Lake Avenue, Toluca Lake

"Well it's this way, Gaucho Bob..."
Bob with Circus Boy producer
Norm Blackburn.

Casey & Friend, Tim Disney
Spreading the News
Casey, left, still at it with CNN.

Class   ...and...   ...clowns

Ooops!

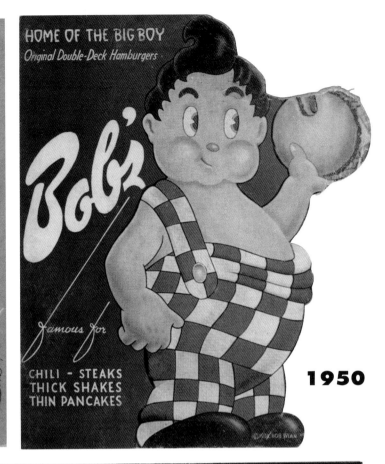

1950

Breakfast Menu - 1964

BIG BOY Executive Conference 1974

BIG BOY Executive Conference 1975

An Asphalt Odyssey

You *can* get your kicks and a big dose of kitsch on
Route 66, where nostalgia and reality meet.

By REED JOHNSON
TIMES STAFF WRITER

DANBY, Calif.—Many miles to the west in the thickening twilight lies Roy's Cafe, a rustic high-desert hangout for weary Route 66 pilgrims, including Ronald Reagan and Harrison Ford (or so the guidebook says). Alas, it's already closed for the night.

Dead ahead, huge lightning bolts crack the sky, casting an eerie pallor over the surrounding moonscape. Suddenly, I feel like Janet Leigh in "Psycho," eyes scanning the rearview mirror, ears straining for those slashing Bernard Hermann chords. As a sheet of rain clatters violently across the windshield, an ominous thought hijacks the brain: Wasn't that a flash-flood warning sign a mile or two back?

This wasn't exactly the Route 66 I'd come looking for, the Route 66 of Howdy Doody-era diners and irresistibly cheesy souvenir stands, a nostalgic slice of pure Americana frozen in amber like some prehistoric insect. Certainly it didn't much resemble the Route 66 depicted in the colorful Automobile Club of Southern California map spread out on the passenger seat beside me, a "greatest hits" anthology of wigwam motels, meteor craters, auto museums and folksier-than-thou truck stops.

No, this lonely, bewitching, exhilarating stretch of asphalt was more akin to what greeted Dust Bowl refugees in the 1930s, who crossed the Colorado River from Arizona, just up the road. After traveling hundreds of miles and enduring heat, cold, hunger, exhaustion and marauding goon squads bent on turning them back, those desperate migrants knew Route 66 as a harshly exotic highway, tinted with beauty and danger, promise and menace. It was "the connection between wherever people were and wherever they wanted to be," as Paul Snyder, director of the newly opened Route 66 Museum in Kingman, Ariz., puts it.

It's this Route 66, a gritty mental Polaroid framed by Walker Evans, that still grips the imagination of thousands of visitors who come here from around the globe every year. And it was this Route 66 that now flashed hypnotically across the stormy landscape, with hardly another human being in sight.

Such trance-inducing solitude may be tougher to find in the coming months. Seventeen years after its last broken fragments were decommissioned by the federal government and left for scavengers, Route 66 has become America's best-known comeback trail. Since the mid-1980s, dozens of books, videos, TV specials and travelogues have celebrated its motley heritage. This year, the 2,448-

Please see Route 66, E3